CW00420499

# Handbook

## Ronan Coghlan

# www.capallbann.co.uk

# Handbook of Fairies

©1998 Ronan Coghlan

ISBN 1 898307 911

First published 1998
Revised edition with new illustrations 1999

## ALL RIGHTS RESERVED

Cover design by Paul Mason
Painting for cover by Marc Potts
Illustrations on pages: 20, 48, 68, 72, 78, 110, 116, 122, 126, 128, 154
and 169 by Marc Potts
Illustrations on pages: 16, 28, 30, 34, 36, 58, 62, 66, 70, 74, 92, 94, 106, 136, 166
and 168 by Daniel Cairns


Published by:

Capall Bann Publishing
Freshfields
Chieveley
Berks
RG20 8TF

Dedication

For Lara, Kieran and Ivona

# Introduction

Fairies or beings analogous to them are found amongst the beliefs of many pre-industrial societies. Folklorists have propounded sundry theories to account for the origin of these beliefs. Fairies, they argue, are the spirits of the dead or the faded gods of former religions or nature spirits or memories of previous populations preserved by later conquerors. These various explanations are by no means mutually exclusive.

Primitive societies often held that everything - not just humans, animals and plants, but even the very rocks and rivers - was alive. Even when they came to realise that the said rocks and rivers were not alive in the same sense they were, they would often feel a spirit or god dwelt within them. Moreover the shamans and magicians of each tribe would work themselves into trance states in which they claimed commerce with a variety of spiritual beings, so our primitive human must have had no doubt that such beings abounded.

The question arose as to where, exactly, these beings dwelt and the more thoughtful of our ancestors seem to have grasped the notion that a great many of these otherworldly beings inhabited what was, in fact, an otherworld - a world adjoining and at times interacting with ours, but, in all its essentials, a different dimension. Here, according to Robert Kirk (1644-92), fairies lived out their lives in a kind of society much like our own, afflicted with the same passions and riven by the same conflicts as beset the human world. These fairies in which Kirk believed could be discerned by those with the Second Sight - a gift which enabled them to see into the fairies' world.

There can be little doubt that many fairies in Celtic lands were once revered as gods by the common people. They were demoted to a lesser status when Christianity became the norm, but they were still believed in. On the other hand, the homesprites of many countries may never have been considered as awesome figures like the Celtic gods. They may have started their careers as local spirits or household gods like the Roman lares; or they may have been considered the spirits of some ancestor of the family or even the spirit of some unfortunate sacrificed when the house was built.

Entrances to the fairy world seem to have been through specific types of places. Thus, for example Gwyn ap Nudd could be reached by climbing Glastonbury Tor[1]. There seems to have been a ritual maze on the sides of the Tor and the treading of this may have been considered the route into fairyland. In Arthurian legend, Lancelot was adopted by a fairy associated with a lake, the sword Excalibur was given to Arthur by the Lady of the Lake and Arthur was carried over water to the otherworldly Isle of Avalon to be healed of his wounds. All this would seem to indicate that entrance to the otherworld was gained by going over or through water and, indeed, one hears accounts of fairy brides who are discovered by their husbands living in lakes: rather than suppose these beings to have led a constant underwater existence, it may be thought that the lake was the portal to the realm of Faerie.

Again, the entrance to fairyland is often depicted as being under a hill. This need not mean that our ancestors held there were many fairylands, one under each hill, but rather that each of the hills in question served as a different gateway to the same fairyland. Some of these hills are barrows, burial mounds, which has led certain folklorists to opine that fairies were identical with the spirits of the dead. Such an argument cannot stand up to the fact that hills which were not barrows were also regarded as doors to fairyland and the people who regarded barrows as such did not know that they were in origin places of sepulture.

However, we cannot altogether separate the notion of a link between the fairies and the dead, as some tales speak of deceased persons being noticed among the fairies. Such a notion may be explained, however, without having to identify the two groups.

**4**

What is quite likely to have occurred here is that many of our forebears reasoned that:

(a) Fairies occupied a spiritual world;

(b) the souls of the dead occupied a spiritual world;

(c) both groups occupied the same spiritual world and were therefore identical.

This is a flawed syllogism as it allows neither for a plurality of spiritual worlds or for a plurality of species within one spiritual world. A new twist has been given to fairy beliefs in the modern era of UFOs. Here theorists - one thinks in particular of Jacques Vallée and John Keel - hold that fairies, aliens and even religious apparitions are part of the same phenomenon. They would argue that in the past people reported sightings of fairies while in the present they interpret the same beings as ufonauts. However, against this it may be argued that reported sightings of fairies have not ceased in modern times and a book by Janet and Colin Bord, scheduled for publication in April, 1997, gives case-histories of such sightings. This is not to say that a fairy could not be mistaken for an alien or vice-versa in a specific instance, but to ascribe the two phenomena entirely to the same source is not warranted by the available evidence. No doubt some would here invoke the saw of Occam to the effect that one should.not multiply entities needlessly : if there is any reality behind fairies and any reality behind ufonauts one can use this principle to argue that the two realities are one. However, there is no reason why this principle should hold true in all circumstances.

Another way of looking at the situation is as follows: *Homo sapiens* is like a man standing upon the brink of an ocean, which represents the Unknown. He has no idea of what may be upon the other side. From time to time, artifacts from beyond the ocean are washed up on the shore. The man looks at them and concludes there is land beyond the ocean where these things come from but he does not know how many lands. These things may come from either one or several countries and he cannot suppose that, just because they all come from across the ocean, they all hale from the same point of origin, By the same token, if we allow for the possible reality of otherworldly beings, fairies and aliens inhabiting the Unknown, it does not follow that they must of necessity be the same kind of being, coming from the same place.

Another theory that was formerly popular is that belief in fairies sprang from memories of primitive peoples supplanted by more advanced races. Such may account for some fairy beliefs but does not necessarily mean that they are the only origins of them. Certainly, the ascription of flint arrowheads to the fairies and their vulnerability to iron might be adduced in favour of such an argument. Forty thousand years ago, Cro-Magnon Man turned up in a Western Europe populated by Neanderthals. We do not know how he viewed these Neanderthals, but it is not impossible that relict Neanderthal populations gave rise to traditions of certain of the wilder inhabitants of faerie, such as satyrs and veds. In Medieval Europe, forest-dwelling wildmen were credited with existence and actual hominoids may lurk behind this belief. A recent book by 1. D. Bayanov[2] shows how such creatures may have contributed to the legend of the rusalka in Eastern Europe.

Is it possible that fairies actually exist? The great body of modern opinion responds with a resounding "No!". But is it really logical to be quite so negative? To say that fairies were once mythical gods and could not therefore exist is not quite as conclusive as it might seem for, if fairies had a real existence, it is by no means unlikely that primitive nations, learning of them, would revere them as deities. Modern pagans might take the view that to say fairies were originally pagan deities is not an argument against their existence at all.

Let us try to consider how we might view the possibility of fairies' existence. As we grow up, society passes on to us what it conceives to be the boundaries of the possible. Thus, while an unschooled child may believe that pigs might fly or tooth-brushes come to life and play the ukulele, he is soon taught by society that such things do not happen.

Society as a whole has evolved firm beliefs regarding where the boundaries of the possible lie. Basically, anything that is foreign to the experience of its average member is considered beyond those boundaries. Thus the man in the street is unlikely to believe in UFOs, ghosts or the Loch Ness Monster, not because he has investigated such things and found them to be unreal, but rather because he himself has never seen anything like them and belief in them is not sufficiently widespread amongst his fellow human beings. One is reminded here of the American farmer, who, on seeing a dromedary, exclaimed "There ain't no such animal". The creature was so far beyond what he thought possible that even seeing wasn't believing.

However, although there is no general belief in the phenomena we have mentioned above, there are strong minority groups that give credence to one or more of them. There are no similarly strong groups that believe in fairies. This is because most of us harbour the impression that fairies are beings of the nursery and therefore less possible even than extra-terrestrials and bigfeet. Thus the vast majority of "educated" people reject belief in fairies as nonsensical and superstitious. But it is opinion, not fact, that says there are no fairies, just as opinion, not fact once held the world to be flat; so could there really be such beings and, if so, how might they fit into the universe as we know it?

According to a theory put forward by David Ash and Peter Hewitt[3], our world may be a dimension within a larger dimension, the latter a possible dwelling place of fairies. While we would be apprehensible to those in the larger dimension, they would not be normally but only in exceptional circumstances, apprehensible to us. E. Bernbaum[4], an orientalist, speaks of a possible "fourth dimension". He says we inhabit a three-dimensional world, but it might be possible to step into the fourth dimension, where we would find ourselves in another three-dimensional world. In fact, he seems to imply that, within the fourth dimension, there might be many three-dimensional worlds. Such worlds might be dwelling places of fairies, though Bernbaum himself is seeking a possible location for the fabled city of Shambhala.

One of the questions which arises with regard to time spent in fairyland is that of the passage of time itself. In tales found from Western Europe to China, persons sojourning in fairyland afterwards discover that, while they have spent but a short time there, a much longer time has elapsed in our world. An explanation for this might be offered in the following fashion. Scientists tell us that we occupy a space-time continuum which started out with the Big Bang. Let us suppose that there is not just one, but a plurality of such continua. The realm of faerie would be in one or more of these. If, by some as yet unknown process, we were to slip from our own continuum into another. we might spend only a short time there yet re-enter our own continuum at a much later - or even much earlier-point in time.

While it is all very well to go theorising about other worlds, have we any reason to infer their existence from experience - in other words, has anyone ever been there and come back to tell the tale, apart from in unverifiable legends. The reaction of someone who found he had stepped into another world and then back again might well be to lie low and say nuffin' like Brer Rabbit (or was it Brer Fox?) in somewhat different circumstances. People who have undergone such experiences are quite likely to remain silent about them lest they be carted off to what is known in politically incorrect circles as the Booby Hatch. Many may have wandered between worlds, but felt unable to regale us with their experiences. Nonetheless, I cite here one such example of apparent inter-world-wandering and would suggest a study of the literature of the paranormal might well yield more.

This example is given by the well-known authoress Elizabeth Goudge in a note on her children's book *Linnets and Valerians* (1964). She tells of a woman she met who, driving across Dartmoor in the evening time, found herself in a "wonderful wood", through which she motored. She had never seen it before and it was gone the next morning. An old man told her one would see such a thing but once in a lifetime. This looks to the present writer as if she had driven right out of this world and into another.

In all, when we consider the realm of Faerie, we should hesitate to attribute it to the mere superstition of our ancestors, on whom we are encouraged to shower unmerited contempt by a world-view which tells us we are constantly making what it terms "progress".

Notes
1. G. Ashe *Avalonian Quest* (London, 1982).
2. D. Bayanov *In the Steps of the Russian Snowman* (Moscow, 1996)
3. D. Ash and P. Hewitt *Science and the Gods* (Bath, 1990).
4. E. Bernbaum *The Way to Shambhala* (Garden City, 1980).

# A

## ADARO

A grotesque kind of merman* in the belief of the Solomon Islanders. An adaro has gills, fins on his feet, a horn like a shark's fin and a prong on his head.

## AFANC

We meet the afanc in *Peredur*, a story in the Welsh *Mabinogion*, a collection of tales compiled in the Middle Ages. Here the hero overcomes the afanc, which seems to be a humanoid creature, as it can fling a spear. In later lore the afanc was considered to be a kind of water monster. There was an afanc in Llyn yr Afanc which was lured from its watery habitat by a maiden and it slept with its claw on her breast. It was bound in iron chains, but, awakening, returned to its pool. The chain was attached to a yoke of oxen and they and a man drew the afanc out. The afanc, being conversationally inclined, assured them that, had it not been for the oxen, their endeavours would not have proven successful. This afanc was not killed, but relocated in another pool. King Arthur was supposed to have defeated an afanc in Llyn Barfog.

What exactly was the afanc? Edward Lhuyd, writing in 1693, opined that it was a beaver. However, this is unlikely, as the afanc has an Irish counterpart and linguistic equivalent in the abhac, which originally signified a water-dwelling spirit, perhaps of the dwarf kind, as in Modern Irish *abhac* means a dwarf. We can infer that the *afanc*, like the *abhac*, was a watery being of otherworldly nature.

## AGOGWE

In Tanzanian folklore, agogwe are diminutive hairy men. They may be identical with the "small red men" said to exist in Uganda and even with the "red hairy men" reported from the faraway Ivory Coast. Bernard Heuvelmans, the noted cryptozoologist, thinks there may be substance behind the legend: that the agogwe may be a race of pygmies or even a surviving population of Australopithecus, a pre-human species generally held to be long extinct.

## AGUANE

Human-sized elf-like beings in the folklore of the north of Italy. They are females, long-haired and beautiful to behold. They have shapeshifting powers. They carry young children on their backs, tossing a breast over the shoulder to suckle them. Their husbands are beings called salvani. Aguane are the guardians of streams.

## ÁINE

An important fairy in Irish lore, her dwelling is in Knockainey, Co Limerick. She was said to be one of the Tuatha Dé Danaan* and an ancestress of the Eoghanacht dynasty of Munster. She was also said to be the mother of Earl Gerald (1338-1398) whose father, finding her swimming in Lough Gur and taking her cloak, had been able to force her to mate with him for, while he had it, she was in his power. There are sundry place-names in Ireland containing the element *Áine*, which may indicate that it was once a common noun signifying a goddess.

## ALBERICH

A dwarf in German legend. The poem *Otnit* in the *Heldenbuch* tells us that the Emperor Otnit espied Alberich beneath a linden tree and thought him a small child. However, no doubt to his considerable surprise, Alberich turned out to be his father and helped him to win the reluctant daughter of the equally reluctant Sultan of Syria as his bride. Elsewhere we are told that Alberich was defeated by the hero Siegfried, who won his cloak of invisibility. Alberich is considered to be the original of the fairy king Oberon.

## ALCINA

A fairy sorceress in the Renaissance Italian poems the *Orlando innamorato* (1495) of Boiardo and the *Orlando furioso* (1516) of

Ariosto. She is presented as the sister of Morgan Le Fay* and turns her former lovers into animals, stones, etc. She captured the hero Astolfo and eventually transformed him into a tree.

## ALGON
The protagonist of a Chippewa or Ojibway tale, he came upon a circular path in the grass. Secreting himself, he beheld a car made of osiers alight on the ground. From it came four fairy-like women who danced in a circle, but who fled in their vehicle when he came towards them.

## ALUX
A race of little people in the folklore of the Maya of Yucatan (Mexico). They are supposed to live in small buildings that are to be found outside Mayan temples. They are credited with magic powers. Behind the tradition of the Alux may lie a race of pygmies as yet unknown to science; but M. Shoemaker, writing in the *Fortean Times* (November, 1996) suggests that belief in them may go back to Auilix, a Mayan god mentioned in the *Popol Vuh*, the religious book of the pagan Maya.

## AMAZONA
The Countess d'Aulnoy in her fairy tale *The Princess Carpillona* (1682) introduces this fairy who presents the princess of the title with flowers having the magical power of making her unrecognisable. Amazona had a magic trumpet which restored the sick to health.

## ANA
Name of the queen of the Fairies* in Gypsy lore. Her name may be connected with Sanskrit *anna* nourishment.

## ANCHO
A kind of homesprite* in Spanish lore. He seems to be of a friendly disposition, for he will chat to the family in whose house he operates, but they fear him as well as like him. The pagan origin of the ancho is perhaps indicated by his dislike of church bells.

## ANDRIANORO

The hero of a tale told by the Malagasies of Madagascar. He wished to marry one of three sisters, fairy-like beings from Heaven, who were wont to come down and swim in a certain lake. He changed himself into several different things with a view to catching one of them and at last succeeded.

## ANDVARI

A dwarf in the *Prose Edda*, an Icelandic work of the 13th Century. The god Loki obtained gold from him to serve as blood money for the murder of the son of Hreidmar. We are told in the *Volsunga Saga* that Andvari had stolen this gold from the gods of the Rhine. Andvari tried unsuccessfully to retain a ring and pronounced a curse on the ring when Loki took it from him. This Andvari seems to have been swimming in a lake in fishy guise. He was apparently a pike. His name means 'watcher'.

## ANNWN

A British Celtic otherworld, which Arthur visited to carry off a cauldron. It is likely to be identified with Avalon*. In the *Mabinogion* Arawn is mentioned as a king in Annwn, but he is not the only one there.

## ANUANIMA

The ruler in Arawak legend of a race who lived above the sky. His subjects would don the outer appearance of birds. One fell in love with a hunter who captured her. She married him and took him to live in Anuanima's aerial realm.

## AOIBHEALL

A fairy woman of Co Clare, Ireland. She is known as far away as Cork. She was supposed to have appeared to Brian Boru, High King of Ireland, before the Battle of Clontarf (1014) and prophesied that the first of his sons whom he saw would succeed him.

## APC'LNIC

These diminutive beings come from the folklore of the Montagnais Indians of Canada. They grow to the height of a man's knee. Like other beings of fairy nature, they will kidnap human children. They can disappear by magic.

## APSARAS

An apsaras is a kind of nymph in Indian mythology, sometimes given to a hero as a reward, but often used to tempt men, in order to keep them from attaining godhood. One of these, Urvasir was born to the sage Naranarayana from his thigh. The gods had sent another apsaras to disturb his meditation, but Urvasi was more beautiful than she, which caused friction amongst the gods, all of whom wanted her hand.

## APSARI

The term used for fairies in the Javanese language of Indonesia.

## APUKU

These diminutive beings are forest spirits in the folklore of the Bush Negroes of Suriname.

## ARAK

A kind of homesprite* found in Cambodia. An arak will live in a tree or in the house itself.

## ARIEL

A spirit, fairy or elemental in Shakespeare's *Tempest* (?1611). He had originally been the servant of the witch Sycorax, who had imprisoned him in the rift of a pine tree, from which Prospero the wizard freed him. Shakespeare may have obtained the name from that of a legendary angel or demon. It has since also been used as a name for supernatural beings.

One John Beaumont believed he was plagued by spirits which he seems to have considered of the fairy nature. He relates this in *A Treatise of Spirits* (1705). One of these spirits, be claims, gave his name as Ariel. The name was that of a sylph in Pope's *Rape of*

14

*the Lock* (1714) and, in modern times, that of the fish-tailed heroine of the Disney film *The Little Mermaid*.

## ASKAFROA
An evil spirit, her name means 'ash-wife' . Sacrifices were made to her on Ash Wednesday in Germany.

## ASRAI
Asrais are water fairies. They live in the West of England, near the Welsh border.

## ATUA
Ancestral and household spirits in Polynesian mythology.

## AVALON
The fairy realm to which King Arthur was taken after his final battle to be healed by Morgan Le Fay*. It was supposed to derive its name from the Welsh word for an apple and it is called the Isle of Apples in Geoffrey of Monmouth's *Vita Merlini* (12th Century). However, it seems to have been actually named from a King Avallo or Avalloc said to reign there. He is almost certainly the same as a character in Welsh pedigrees called Afallach, son of the god Beli Mawr. This Afallach was the father of Modrron, who was herself in origin the goddess Matrona from whom apparently the character of Morgan Le Fay emerged. On Avalon it was always springtime, crops grew without the aid of man and none sickened or grew older. It was identified with Glastonbury in Somerset, perhaps because Glastonbury Tor was considered a portal of the otherworld. Avalon was probably identical with Annwn*.

## AWD GOGGIE
A haunter of the woods and orchards of northern England. He was regarded as an evil being.

## AYANA
Spirits amongst the Galla or Oromo of Ethiopia said to live in a sort of paradise.

*Baba Yaga*

# B

## BABA YAGA

A horrid supernatural female in Russian folklore. She lives in a hut with chickens' legs attached to give it mobility. She has stone teeth and breasts. Human flesh figures in her diet. She stirs up storms, which shows she may be, in origin, some kind of weather goddess. She is sometimes part of a dyad or triad of beings.

## BAGAN

A diminutive being in Eastern European folklore who looks after the animals on a farm. Bagans are small and hairy.

## BANNIK

A spirit in Slavic lore who inhabits a bath house. He himself performs his ablutions after nightfall - intrude at your peril. He is of small stature.

## BANSHEE

(Irish *bean sí* woman of the fairies). A spirit in Irish lore which attaches itself to families. Its loud lamentations foretell a death in its family. As to its origins, it is sometimes called *badhbh* in Irish and, as a proper noun, this is the name of a goddess in Irish mythology, a lover of death, and, if before a battle you saw her washing your spoils or the butchered parts of bodies, defeat would befall you. The banshee may have developed from some such goddess.

## BARABAO

In Venetian folklore, a diminutive being, wearing a red cap and capable of shapeshifting. In his natural form, he is quite plump.

# BARGUEST

A frightening spectre in English lore with glowing red eyes, believed in in the north of England. It usually appeared in animal, but sometimes in human form. One near Darlington variously appeared as a headless man, a headless woman, a white cat etc. Barguests sometimes appear in canine form. A barguest in the form of a mastiff was once to be seen regularly in Newcastle. It would prowl about the streets at night howling unpleasantly. The barguest usually has a chain, which clanks in approved ghostly fashion. It can also have claws or horns. The origin of the word has been the subject of some discussion.

# BEAN-NIDHE

(Gaelic, literally 'washerwoman') An otherworldly being in Scottish lore who can be seen at night, washing the shrouds of those who will die. She has much the same function as the *badhbh* of Irish tradition who can be seen before a battle, washing the spoils or limbs of those who will fall.

# BEFANA

(Italian, corrupted form of *Epifania*) A benevolent being in Italian lore. She is an old woman who places gifts for children in their stockings on the Eve of Epiphany. According to legend, she was invited to accompany the Magi on their journey to see Jesus, but claimed she was too busy with housework. She now seeks Jesus each year.

# BENDITH Y MAMAU

Obscure Welsh fairies associated with music and the abduction of children.

# BERCHTE

A fairy being in Germanic lore, probably a goddess in origin, perhaps identical with Holda*. At any rate, where Holda was not found, Berchte, whose name signifies 'the bright one', took her place. Like Holda, she went about between Christmas and the New Year. The name *Holdaberta*, apparently a combination of Holda and Berchte, was sometimes used for her. At her feast gruel and fish were eaten. Those who spun were under her particular supervision: spinning unfinished at the end of the year she destroyed.

## BIG GREY MAN

An entity reported to exist on Ben Macdhui in the Cairngorms. Wide knowledge of him first spread when mountaineer Norman Collie claimed that in 1895 on the mountain he heard crunching noises behind him and was then overcome with fear.

It was said he also claimed to have seen a large, grey figure, but this is probably a later addition to the story. There are various rumours about the Big Grey Man and he seems to be a genuine being of folklore, as he has a Gaelic name (*Fear Liath Mor*).

## BILBERRY MAN

A kind of evil spirit of the forest in German lore. To stop him attacking you, you had to leave an offering of bread and fruit on a stone before entering the forest.

## BINDICA

Beauteous fairies in Sicily. They have the power to make themselves invisible and therefore are rarely seen.

## BIRD SIMER

The father of a fairy-like being in Kurdish tradition. She could fly around garbed in the outer appearance of a bird. She was captured by a giant, but rescued by two heroes. She married one of these, but eventually donned her bird skin and feathers and flew home.

## BLACK ANNIS

A hag in English folklore. She had a blue face and cattle and children formed part of her diet. She lived in a cave which she hollowed out with her nails in the Dane Hills. There was formerly a ceremony in her honour in which a hunt pursued a dead cat dragged ahead of it. Indications are that Black Annis was originally a goddess. Her name has been likened to that of

*Black Annis*

the Irish goddess Ana, who was perhaps worshipped in Britain under the name of Dôn, but any connection here is conjectural.

## BLOODY-BONES

An evil kind of goblin* used to terrify children in Somerset. He was said to live in a cupboard, surrounded by the bones of recalcitrant children on whom he had feasted, his face festooned with blood. Children dared not look through the cupboard's keyhole, as this was supposed to lead to capture by the creature.

## BLUE BURCHES

A Somerset spirit who was supposed to have lived in a shoemaker's house on the Blackdown Hills. Though his actual appearance was that of an oldster caparisoned in blue trousers, he could change his shape. Two clergymen were said to have driven him away.

## BLUE MAIDENS

(Finnish *Sinipiiat*) Beings in Finnish belief who look after the flowers.

## BLUE MEN OF THE MINCH

In Scottish lore, supernatural beings that were found in the sea. They had long, grey faces and were up to the waist in water. They seem to be a personification of the sea itself.

## BOCAN

A kind of goblin* or spectre, not necessarily of evil intent, found in Scotland.

## BOCKMANN

A goat-man of German lore, of an evil character.

## BOCKSCHITT

Another name for the *pilwiz**

## BOGGART

A kind of homesprite* attached to a family. It would sometimes help with tasks about the farm, but could also be something of a menace, annoying the family. A boggart was sometimes thought of as a ghost or even a malignant spirit. One well-known boggart, lacking a head, was known in Preston. Despite its handicap, it walked about the streets until it was exorcised. The term boggart was also applied to a creature with a small boat, reported on the River Trent. It had phocine features and long hair and was of small stature.

In 1867 there was a boggart living at Syke Lumb Farm near Blackburn. He would at times help around the farm, but, if he became angry with the humans, he could cause considerable annoyance.

## BOGEY

A generally frightening creature. In the 19th Century, the Bogey was a term for the Devil, used when speaking to children.

## BOGLE

A being, ill-defined, unpleasant and evil, black in colour. The bogle may once have had a specific definition, but it does not seem to be remembered. The true English form of the word is the dialect *boggle*, but *bogle* became the standard English word when introduced to the literary language by Scottish writers. In Scotland March 29th was formerly alluded to as Bogle Day but the reason for this is lost.

## BORUTA

In Polish folklore, a kind of spirit which inhabits a fir.

## BROLLACHAN

A naked or ragged hirsute being in Scottish folklore, the brollachan was essentially shapeless. Lewis Spence thinks the brollachan was the same as the fuath*

# BROUNGER

A sea-spirit said to dwell off the east coast of Scotland. He seems to have been connected with bad weather and may have been a thunder god in origin.

## BROWN, JANE

In a tale related as true by James Hogg (1770-1835), this Scottish girl disappeared as a child and a great but fruitless search was made for her. The minister at Innerleithar persuaded seven congregations to pray for her safe return on one Sunday and within an hour she was found by a wood. She had apparently been well fed and there was a tinge of blue on her skin. The people at the time suggested she had been taken by the pixies*. Jane lived to a ripe old age.

## BROWNIE

A sprite in the folklore of Scotland. It is similar to, but was probably originally different from, the Highland sprite called an urisk*. The brownie was shaggy and its clothing, when it wore clothing, for sometimes it went naked, was coloured with the brownness which gave it its name. Latterly a diminutive being, it seems at first to have been human-sized or bigger. It was sometimes said to be noseless, sometimes without fingers and toes. It did tasks around the home and farm and used to be paid with offerings of milk. If offered clothes, it would depart. It appeared from the hearth*. Its protection extended to the family it served, rather than the mere building in which it worked. In the Peninsular war (1808-14), the brownie of the McKays was said to have accompanied the chief, protecting him from French bullets. It has been suggested that the brownie was an ancestral spirit and that it was analogous to the lar, the household god of the ancient Romans. However brownies did not always regard the house in which they lived as their home: they would have an outside permanent residence, such as a pool or a cave. Brownies flourished in the Lowlands of Scotland, perhaps only in later times penetrating the Highlands to any extent. Scottish immigration brought them to Northern Ireland. The brownie was also known in the north of England. Belief in the brownie was brought to North America by the colonists.

## BRYN-YR--ELLYLON

A fairies' well near Mold (Wales). Workmen dug it up in 1833 to discover a skeleton, that of a tall man wearing a golden collar or cape - though how a cape is supposed to have survived we are not told. A story after the event said that an old woman some time before had seen a tall figure wearing a golden coat which shone like the sun in the darkness of the night crossing the road nearby.

## BUCCA

A kind of spirit in Cornish folklore. Two buccas are believed in, the Bucca Gwidden (White Bucca) and the Bucca Dhu (Black Bucca). The former was good, the latter evil. We may have here a reminiscence of two gods in a dualistic system. The bucca was also called a Bucca-Boo cf. English *bugaboo*, a kind of goblin, Welsh *bwcibo*, devil.

## BUCKY

A being thought to exist in the Lowlands of Scotland. He would leap onto a horse behind its rider and garrot him.

## BUG

An ill-defined being of the night which caused terror, used as a threat to frighten children.

## BUGABOO

An evil spirit. The origin of the term is obscure, perhaps from Welsh *bwcibo* (devil). *Buglebo* seems to be a variant of the word. There may be a connection with Bugibus, a demon in the literature of medieval France.

## BUGBEAR

A creature similar to the bug* mentioned above, used to hush children. The *Oxford English Dictionary* (2nd ed.) opines, not unreasonably, that it was originally in bear form.

## BUJANGGA

A bujangga is a gigantic angel-like being in the mythology of the Sunda Islands (Indonesia).

## BULL-BEGGAR

A frightening spirit or spectre, which presumably originally was in taurine form. A particular bull-beggar was said to abide at Creech Hill in Somerset.

## BWBACH

A Welsh fairy, perhaps identical with the pwca*.

# C

## CACCE-HALDE
Spirit of the water in Lappish lore.

## CAILLEACH BEARA, CAILLEACH BHEUR
A supernatural hag in Gaelic folklore; the first is the Irish form of her name, the second the Scottish. She originated from the Beare Peninsula in South-West Ireland, hence her name ('Hag of Beare'). Her personal name was *Boi*, which indicates that she was associated with cattle (Irish *bó*, a cow). Although depicted as an old woman, she had gone through various periods of youth. When young and beautiful, she seems to have been associated with kings and this would indicate she was originally a goddess of the sovereignty of the land. She had two sisters - a goddess splitting into a triad is familiar to students of Irish mythology. In Connacht, she was associated with the harvest. In Scotland, she seems to have been a goddess of winter and the second part of her name was associated with Gaelic *beur*, cutting. Her face was blue-black, her hair the colour of frozen twigs. She had a single eye and lived upon Ben Nevis, sometimes riding storm clouds with other hags in attendance. She was accompanied by animals: deer, goats, sheep, pigs and wolves. She had a basket of earth from which she was said to have made Scotland. Earth and stones which dropped from her basket became the Hebrides. A rock which fell through a hole in her apron became Ailsa Craig. She had two sons one white, the other black with a white spot on his breast. She would fight against Spring and, each year when Spring came, she would throw her staff under a holly tree, where no grass would grow subsequently. She was overthrown each March 25th. It was said that each year her son married the Summer Maid. She tried each March and April to hold off Summer with awful weather. Her son would chase her north and take her single eye.

# CALLICANTZAROS

This creature is found in modern Greek folklore. Callicantzaroi are said to appear only between Christmas and Epiphany, when they go careering by. They vanish at the third cock crow. Their leader is sometimes ithyphallic. The rest of the year they are in the Underworld, gnawing the tree that supports the world. When they are above ground, this tree re-grows. Sometimes it is said they are merely men who have been changed into callicantzaroi. If you thrust a flaming torch into the face of a callicantzaros, it will supposedly turn back into a human. (If it doesn't, you are likely to have a mightily piqued callicantzaros on your hands). In Cyprus they are called Planetaroi. Descriptions of this creature vary wildly. Some of them are gigantic, hairy, bald, red-eyed and black faced with large heads and genitalia. Some are short and sturdy. Sometimes they have tusks, talon-like fingers, ears of a donkey or goat or long tails. They can have goat horns, the legs of a goat or donkey, one human and one animal leg or human legs with feet twisted backwards. Some are pygmies, black of hue and hairless. These latter ride beasts that resemble themselves or roosters, small horses or large donkeys. Their noses, hands and feet may be askew and they may be one-eyed. In one locality callicantzaroi were reported as being merely savage men.

# CARABOSSE

The name of the wicked fairy in Tchaikovski's *Sleeping Beauty* (1890). It means a hunchback.

# CATEZ

A kind of sprite in Slavic lore. Like the Greek god Pan, his upper portion resembles a human, the lower a goat.

# CAYFOR

A kind of goblin*, said to frequent the forests of Brazil. In Brazilian lore, he is somewhat akin to the nursery bogle*. He has red hair and his skin is red.

*Callicantzaros*

# CENTAUR

Centaurs were creatures in Greek mythology. They had human bodies down to the waist, where they were joined onto a horse's four-legged body. The Greeks in fact distinguished between three kinds of centaur - the hippocentaur (human/horse), the onocentaur (human/donkey) and the ichthyocentaur, whose form has not been preserved but, from its name, it must have had fishy parts. Centaurs were generally depicted as wild and uncouth, though an exception was Chiron, who served as tutor to Hercules and Jason. Another well-known centaur was Nessus, who brought about the death of Hercules. Some Greeks said that centaurs were descendants of Centaurus son of Ixion, who copulated with horses. Depictions of centaurs predate the Greeks and are found in the Near East on boundary markers made by the Kassites, who irrupted into that region in the Second Millenium BC. John Mandeville, whose *Travels* (1356-7) is a literary hoax, mentions a race of man-eating centaurs called ypotains. Aldrovandi's *Historia Monstrorum* (1642) shows an illustration of a centaur with no forelegs, who still manages to stand upright, despite the constraints of Newtonian physics. Countess d'Aulnoy, the famed French writer of fairy tales, featured the Blue Centaur, who was part man and part goat, in *The Princess Carpillona* (1682).

# CHANGELING

Belief in changelings was widespread in Europe. A changeling is a being of fairy nature left in place of a human child. Shakespeare in *A Midsummer Night's Dream* misuses the term to mean the child which has been stolen. Changelings may be recognised by their precocity, by their big heads, by their big teeth and appetites and by their liking for music. It is likely that children with all manner of deformities and handicaps were suspected of being changelings in days gone by.

There were various measures taken to prevent children being replaced by changelings. Baptism protected a child, as did iron, repugnant to fairies. At the time of birth, nine pieces of blanket or plaid could be put on a woman to keep the fairies away. A Bible or a piece of the mother's wedding garment placed beneath

*Centaur*

30

her pillow were effective deterrents. You could burn an old shoe, in the knowledge that the fairies would not come near because of the smell. Burning the afterbirth or putting a live coal or gold coin into the baby's first bath were thought to protect it. If the father stayed in the house, the fairies would not comer or so it was said in Leitrim (Ireland), while in the Isle of Man the father's trousers left on the bed provided the same result. Once you discovered your baby had been replaced by a changeling, how did you get it back? It was necessary to make the changeling return to Faerie. You could do that by putting it to work or placing it on a dungheap or a hot shovel. To make sure that a child was in fact a changeling, some strategy was needed to trick him into speaking. This could be done by taking some unusual action to excite his astonishment, leading him to comment, such as fermenting beer in an eggshell, making a pudding with the skin still on, or something similar.

## CHING

Diminutive human beings in Chinese lore. They are 9" tall and live in the land of Hsiao-jen ko. In origin they may be of learned rather than folkloric origin.

## CHURCH GRIM

A homesprite* found in a church; called *Kirkgrim* in German, *Kyrkogrim* in Swedish and *Kirkegrim* in Danish.

## CIN

In Turkish lore, this is a spirit that can appear in any of a number of shapes, as a dwarf, giant or animal. In cities cins can be found in rubbish dumps. They occupy a variety of places in the countryside and are normally invisible. Men call them by the term *onlar* ('they'). They can be either friendly or unfriendly, male or female. Their system of government is monarchical.

## CHURCHES

In Warwickshire folklore, fairies are on two occasions credited with selecting the location of churches. At Knowle, the fairies had removed stones from the place where the builders had started their work and placed them on a new site, where the building was eventually finished. Much the same happened at Warmington.

## CIUTHACH
A savage being in Scottish folklore, perhaps identical with the urisk*.

## CLINT'S CRAGS
These rocks at Weardale, Co Durham, contain a cave which was said to be the location of a fairy court, presided over by the Queen of the Fairies.

## CLIONA
A fairy woman in Irish legend. She was said to live in a subterranean palace in Co Cork. One story makes her a sister of Aoibheall*. In an early tale, she was drowned at Glandore.

## CLURICAUNE
This is the name of a diminutive being in Irish folklore. It is perhaps, but by no means certainly, identical with the leprechaun*. Cluricaunes are to be found in wine-cellars, drinking. They harness and race sheep, goats and sheepdogs.

## COBLYNAU
Welsh mine fairies, said to be dwarfs about 18" high. They sometimes, however, can appear larger - this has been noted when they were outside. Sometimes they use handkerchiefs as headdresses and wear red jackets, but more often they seem to be clad in garb reminiscent of miners'. They worked in fairy mines and sometimes, when their labours were overheard, humans would discover ore there but afterwards the coblynau would work there no more.

## COCHION
Literally, the Red Ones (Welsh *coch*, red), a race of fairy type known fully as *Y Gwyllied Cochion*, the Red Fairies. They lived in a forest called Coed y Dugoed Mawr, used stone arrows and did not dwell in houses. There are said to have been some alive

as late as the 19th Century, though a great many of them are supposed to have been hanged in 1534 by a Baron Owen, who was later slain by some of the angered survivors. They were feared by the people round about, who put scythes in their chimneys to keep them from entering their cottages.

## COCO, EL

Amongst groups of Hispanic origin, a being used to threaten crying babies who will not cease making noise. El Coco is, in a rather racist way, depicted as black and it is said he will eat troublesome offspring.

## CORN-BUCK

(German *Kornböck*) A kind of spirit that lives in cornfields and appears to humans in various animal guises. He is often invisible. He can assume the appearance of a cornflower and, as such, pass unnoticed.

## CORRIGAN

Corrigans are diminutive beings in Breton lore, sometimes referred to as *nains* (dwarfs*). They are not very well disposed towards humans, as is indicated by the fact that they are at war with the lutins*, because the lutins are too human-friendly. Corrigans like dancing in circles. Mushrooms grow where corrigans danced. They wear linen cloth, white in colour and rough of texture. They live under dolmens.

## CORWRION

A pool, said to be bottomless, near Bethesda, North Wales. The fairies are said to live beneath its waters. They could be seen dancing or mowing hay nearby in former days.

## COTTINGLEY FAIRIES

These fairies were supposedly photographed in the early part of the 20th Century. Two cousins, Frances Griffiths and Elsie Wright, first claimed they had seen the fairies and.then produced alleged photographs of them. They attained a certain fame. Sir Arthur Conan Doyle believed they were genuine and no one

*Corrigan*

succeeded in proving they had been faked. Then in 1981 Frances confessed that four of the five photographs had been faked, while Elsie asserted that none of them were genuine. However, both maintained that they had really seen fairies in Cottingley. Others too have claimed to have seen fairies there.

## CRAIG-Y-DDINAS
Rock in wales which fairies are still said to inhabit.

## CRYMLYN LAKE
A lake in South Wales peopled by fairies. It is said that some people had annoyed St Patrick, so he turned the men into fish and the women into fairies in the lake.

## CWM LLWCHI, LLYN
Lake in Powys, believed to contain an invisible island on which the fairies had a garden. There was a door in a rock by the lake and, on May Day, this would open, so one could go by a subterranean passage to the island. However, this possibility ceased when someone took a flower from the island.

## CWMSILINI, LLYN
Lake in North Wales where little people, about a foot tall, were reported dancing and jumping to the accompaniment of strange music.

## CYCLOPS
The cyclopses or cyclopes were a race of giants in classical mythology. Each cyclops sported a single eye in the centre of his forehead. The most famous tale involving a cyclops is told by Homer in the *Odyssey*. The hero, Odysseus (called Ulysses by the Romans) landed on the island of the cyclops with his crew. They came to the cave of a cyclops called Polyphemus, who confined the hapless mariners in his abode and proceeded to eat a couple at each mealtime. Odysseus in due course escaped by blinding Polyphcmus with a stake.

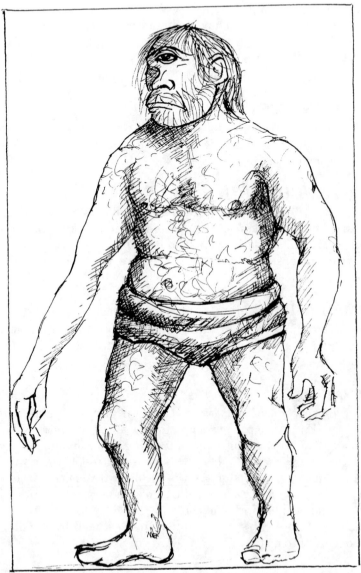

*Cyclops*

Poor Polyphemus didn't seem to have much luck - he fell in love with a nymph* named Galatea, but his passion was unrequited, presumably one-eyed primitive giants weren't her type.

The Greeks believed that cyclopes constituted a species and the island on which they dwelt was generally identified with Sicily, where in modern times there is a cave called La Grotta di Polifimo. This has led to the suggestion that Polyphemus was a personification of Mount Etna. However, it must be remembered that an actual race of cyclopes was supposed to exist and a possible explanation of this is that huge, human-looking skulls with what appear to be central eye-sockets, have been discovered on the island. These skulls are in fact those of prehistoric elephants and the 'eye-sockets' are nasal openings. (The real eye-sockets are at the side).

Hesiod said the cyclopes were but three in number and this may indicate that they were in origin a mythical one-eyed trio whose name was later given to a race of one-eyed giants whose supposed remains the ancients discovered. Cyclopean beings are found in legends outside Greece. Sinbad the sailor encountered one on his travels and the Basques had a legendary one-eyed giant called Tartaro. In the tales of the Oghuz Turks there is a menacing cyclops called Tepegoz while ghouls are cyclopean in the beliefs of the Sahara. Chinese geographical lore knew of a race of human-sized cyclopeans that lived in the land of I-nu Kuo.

## CYHIRAETH
A kind of spirit in Welsh lore. She has tangled locks, long black teeth, wings which she flaps against the window and shrivelled arms. She comes to the window of a dying person, calling him. She will tell a wife if her husband is to die, or a husband if his wife is to die.

## CYNWCH, LLYN
Lake in North Wales which is said to have fairy inhabitants beneath it. A folktale has a man who fell in remaining with the fairies for a month or thereabouts.

# D

## DAHARI
These were the offspring of a jinn* named Sakhar who had built
Baladu Nuhasir, a copper or brazen city, in Africa.

## DAKINI
A malevolent being in Indian lore, noted for the  drinking of
blood.

## DARK MAN
(Irish *fear dorcha*) A messenger sent by the fairy queen to bring
mortals to her. If they return and reveal fairy secrets, the Dark
man withers one of their limbs or removes the eye with the fairy
vision.

## DANAMO
A fairy in the Countess d'Aulnoy's *Fairy Tales* (1682). Her
daughter Azira loved Prince Parcinus, but he was in love with
Irolta. Danamo tried unsuccessfully to make Irolta marry a fairy
called Brutus, but Parcinus foiled her designs and Azira ended
up marrying Brutus.

## DAUGHTERS OF THE SUN
Strange females said to inhabit an island in the Okeefenokee
Swamp in the southern U.S.A. They are said to have musical
voices and angelic faces, though whether they are other-worldly
beings or simply part of a lost race of humans cannot be inferred
from the legends. According to a Creek Indian tradition, they
brought certain white hunters, whom they found sick, to their
island and cured them, but then transported them away in a
cloud of smoke. The hunters entered the swamp once again, but
disappeared. The sound of the laughter of the Daughters of the

Sun or glimpses of their forms, which are said to shimmer, are said to have been experienced by wayfarers.

## DAVY JONES

A nautical spirit, said to warn sailors of impending doom. Once drowned, they are imprisoned in Davy Jones's Locker, beneath the waves. He is possibly of Celtic origin, his very name bearing a Welsh stamp.

## DEAD

In some fairy tales it would seem that fairies are identified with the dead; but this should not be taken as proof positive that they were ghosts in origin as, in folklore, different kinds of spirit are easily confused and categories are not strictly adhered to.

## DEMOGORGON

A mysterious being who, according to Ariosto, lived in the Himalayas and at whose palace, every fifth year, the fairies had to appear. Spenser places him in an abyss with the Fates. His origin is obscure. Medieval annotators on the classics mention him, the scholiast on Statius saying he was a great underworld god who was called upon in magical ceremonies. In Conrad de Mare's *Repertorium* (1273) he is called the earliest deity of mythology.

## DERRICK

A term used in Devon, apparently synonymous with pixy[*]

## DEVA

Among the Hindus, devas were gods, while the Persians classed them as demons, followers of Ahriman. In modern times the term is used to mean a nature spirit.

## DIRNE-WEIBEL

A female woodland sprite in Bavarian folklore. She dressed in red and would carry a basket of apples. She would give these away and they would turn into money. She would ask people she encountered to go with her. If they didn't, she would cry.

## DOBIE

A being in West Yorkshire belief who will jump up behind a horseman and garrot him. Dobies are unintelligent. They live in farmhouses, byres, granges and near old towers and bridges.

## DOCKIN, TOM

An iron-toothed being in the lore of the north of England. His victims are children.

## DOGIR

A race of underwater spirits in the folklore of Northern Sudan. They live in the Nile. Occasionally they will kidnap human women. In certain areas they are looked on as monstrous beings.

## DOMOVOY

A kind of homesprite* found in the east of Europe. Domovoys live in stoves. They are small in stature and very hairy.

## DÖPPELGANGER

Robert Kirk* says that he was informed by those with second sight that each man has one of these in the fairy realm who exactly resembles him. This double-man may be seen both before and after the man he resembles is dead.

## DRAC

A water dwelling being in French lore. Gervase of Tilbury gives what he claims is a true account of an encounter with dracs, for he claims he met the woman concerned. She was, she told him, taken to live under water by a drac to nurse his child; but she couldn't see well until one day she smeared her eye with grease from an eel pasty. When she had returned to the human world, one day she saw the drac and greeted him. He asked her with which eye she could see him. It was, of course, the eye onto which she had put the grease. The drac poked her in the eye with his finger and disappeared.

## DRUIDS

Priests or wizards of the Celtic religion. In Wales it was believed that fairies were the souls of good druids, while the Cornish held that fairies were druids who had shrunk because they would not give up their beliefs.

## DUENDE

A diminutive being in Spanish folklore, the duende has shapeshifting and invisibility powers. Active at night, duendes like to wake up sleepers. The duende seems to be a homesprite* in origin, as the term is derived from Spanish *duen de casa* (lord of the house). A duende, which appears like an old man or a small boy, can be helpful as well as harmful. The duende has been exported to the American continent, where it is found in the folklore of Belize. Duendes in Belize are supposed to be little men, sometimes dressed in skins. They wear large hats. The duende is known familiarly as Tata (Grandpa) Duende.

## DULLAHAN

A species of being in Irish lore that rides about on a headless horse. He carries his own head under his arm. Wherever he stops, someone dies.

## DUNTER

A being in Scottish lore. One finds dunters in old castles and peel-towers. A dunter will strike flax or barley in a hollow stone. Prolonged and loud sounds caused by this activity foretold death or ill-luck. Dunters are also called powries.

## DWARF

(plural dwarfs) Dwarfs occur in Germanic mythology and the word has various cognates in the Teutonic languages, e.g., German *zwerg*, Anglo-Saxon *dweorg*, Dutch *dwerg*, Danish *dverg*, etc. Dwarfs would seem to be identical with the Black Elves (*svartâlfar*) mentioned by the Icelandic writer Snorri Sturluson (1178–1241) and this would explain why some dwarfs have the element *alf* (elf) in their names. Dwarfs are largely involved with smithcraft. A dwarf is grown up at the age of three and has a grey beard at seven. The dwarf is a hunchback, wearing rough clothing. Sometimes his non-humanity is emphasised by his having the feet of a goose or a duck. Dwarfs live in a hole (*gauri*) in the rocks. They are also found under houses or barns, in mountains, grave-mounds or cairns. They can be thievish, stealing from pea-fields. A hat or cloak which renders them invisible is sometimes part of their attire. According to the Heldenbuch, dwarfs had the following origin: Because much gold and silver, precious stones and pearls were in the mountains and because the mountains were wasteland, God made the dwarfs to inhabit them.

On the island of Rügen (Germany) it was believed there were three kinds of dwarfs: White Dwarfs largely lived beneath the hills in winter, but frisked about on summer nights. They were allowed out by day only singly and in another form, e.g., a bird or a butterfly. Brown Dwarfs were very small. They had caps which made them invisible to all those not wearing caps of the same sort. They had the power to be shapeshifters. Black dwarfs were ugly, evil, mischievous and good at smithcraft. These three kinds of dwarfs were called from the colour of their clothes.

In Brittany the term dwarf (*nain*) is sometimes used to mean a corrigan*, sometimes one of a hairy species of unpleasant appearance.

## DZIWITZA
A female spirit in Polish folklore. She is a huntress and carries a zylba, which, as every schoolboy knows, is a species of javelin. She is a beautiful princess, accompanied by excellent hounds. If you were in the forest at midday, Dziwitza would appear to you. scaring the liver out of you.

# E

## EACHRAIS URLAIR

Gaelic, 'mischief of the floor*. The name of a specific female of the fairy kind in Scots lore. She was associated with discord and could turn people into animals with a magic wand. She was normally to be seen sitting on her hunkers. She dwelt near the palaces of kings, whose children would use her abode as a place of assignation.

## EAGER

Apparently a name given to a water spirit in the River Trent. When the water was in flood, bargees would say to one another that Eager was coming. Eager may have been a god in origin, such as the Norse Aegir.

## EARLY, BIDDY

(died 1873) Irish prophetess. She could see the fairies and had powers of healing, which she used for the good of both people and animals. She could also see into the future. Some of her work was effected by the use of a blue bottle, which she had been given by the fairies. Before her death, she had this bottle thrown into a lake.

## EARTHMAN

A term applied to an elf- or dwarf-like being in part of Germany.

## EDENHALL LUCK

An enamelled glass which was said to have been found by a servant of the Musgrave family. When he came upon it, fairies were dancing around it. He picked it up and the fairies sang out that if the glass should break or fall, the luck of Edenhall would depart. The Musgrave family kept the Luck of Edenhall, as the glass was called, for hundreds of years. It is now in the Victoria and Albert Museum.

## ELEMENTAL
A term used to mean an otherworldly being made up of one element only.

## ELF
A term signifying a diminutive being in Germanic mythology; the English word comes from Anglo-Saxon *aelf*, which has numerous cognates in the Teutonic languages, e.g., Old Norse *âlfr*, Old High German *alp*, etc. It may originally have meant a white spirit of goodly bent, cf. Latin *albus*, Sabine *alpus*, 'white', perhaps ultimately connected with Sanskrit *ribhu*, 'shining'. Certainly they were regarded as beings which shone. J.R.R. Tolkien (*On Fairy Tales*) has argued that elves were originally of human stature, their diminutive stature being a later development. The Anglo-Saxon term denoted a fairy generally and in Scots this usage persists and in Scottish lore fairies are considered to be of human height. However, this does not prove that all continental elves have shrunk from former loftiness. In Spenser (*Faerie Queene*) elves are male fairies and fays female ones and they are given human size.

The elves were grouped by the Norse with the Aesir. a race of gods, and this gave them at least quasi-divine status. The Norsemen may not have really distinguished between elves and gods as two gods, Loki and Volund,, are actually called elves. The relationship between elves and dwarfs* is perhaps a little difficult to define. That there was possibly an overlap between the two concepts is indicated by the fact that some dwarfs have elf names, such as Alfr and Vindalfr. Snorri Sturluson (1178-1241) divides the elves into light elves (*liosâlfar*), dark elves (*döckâlfar*) and black elves (*svartâlfar*). The last-mentioned he identifies with dwarfs. In modern Norwegian folklore, a distinction between elf and dwarf is maintained.

Light elves lived either in Alfheim or in the third space of heaven. Alfheim was held to be under the roots of Yggdrasil, the world tree of Norse mythology. Elves were held to have the power of invisibility. They were tricksy and thievish and would tangle the hair of people and horses. They had the ability to turn into butterflies and into the boughs of alder, aspen or willow. They were ruled by kings and queens. They lived under houses and were very fond of music and dancing. They were said to have a subterranean rose-garden where you could not pick the flowers. Elves were said to marry, multiply and at length grow old and die. In Danish lore, male elves looked like old men with low-crowned hats, whereas females were beautiful and would play on instruments which would lure men to them, but they were hollow behind.

Elves liked to dance in the moonlight and they could prophesy. Elves were sometimes associated with disease. It was said they would shoot men and beasts with their arrows, causing death. They were thought to spread disease also, for example, the water-elf disease, which may have been chicken-pox. In Danish lore, elf men would sunbathe, but, if you went up to one and he breathed on you, you would fall ill.

The question arose, after the introduction of Christianity, as to how elves fitted into the Christian world-view. The dour Scots opined that they were descended from Satan. Other theories were that God made them without parents; or that they were descended from a race of non-Adamite men, either coeval with or previous to the Adamites. According to one view, they were descended from Adam before his union with Eve. We are reminded here of the Hebrew legend that, before the creation of Eve, Adam had a wife called Lilith. They are also described as Eve's hidden children. As to whether they had souls, some said they had, others that they merely had breath. The elves would have drowned in the Flood, but God put them safely in a cave.

Elves may have been originally minor divinities or nature spirits. To some extent they may have been considered the souls of the dead.

## ELF-SHOT

Flint arrowheads were formerly ascribed in country districts to the work of elves*. With their arrows it was believed that    elves would shoot humans and animals alike. No wound would be discernable on the skin of the victim, but death would follow. A number of folk remedies were prescribed for the cure of elf- shot.

## ELIDOR

The name of a Welsh priest whose extraordinary story is told by Giraldus Cambrensis (12th-13th Century). When Elidor was a boy he hid one day rather than attend school and was found by two diminutive beings, who invited him to their country, to which they took him by means of a tunnel. This led to a land where there were meadows, woods and streams, but where the sky was always overcast. They had no moon or stars by night. Elidor was made welcome by the pygmy inhabitants of the country, their king among them. The folk there ate neither meat nor fish, but only milk dishes. They revered truth highly. The boy lived in the country, but would return from time to time to visit his mother. She besought him to bring her something gold from the country, as gold was in abundance there. He stole a golden ball, but thereafter he could never find his way back. As an adult he became a priest. Giraldus (not always a reliable historian) says he always asserted the story was true; indeed, he would weep at the memory of its events. The little people spoke a language of their own, some words of which were *ydor* (water) and *halgein* (salt).

## ELIMA

(plural *bilima*) Spirits believed in by the Mongo-Nkundo peoples of Congo. They are connected with fertility. They live in rivers, marshes and trees.

## ELLYLLON

Ugly and diminutive beings in Welsh folklore. The term is sometimes translated as 'elves'

## ELOKO

A kind of unpleasant otherworldly being believed in in Congo. The plural is *biloko*. Some are giants* with crocodilian jaws, some powerful-handed dwarfs*. Sometimes they are said to be hairless, growing grass instead. They live in hollow trees and leaves form their sole apparel.

## EQQO

Spirits in the belief of the Kafa of Ethiopia. They dwell in wild places and are credited with the powers to possess someone, who would then speak oracularly.

## EXOTICA

Another name for a nereid* (modern sense).

*Fairy*

# F

## FACHAN

A strange being in Scottish lore, having a tuft on his head and his hand sticking out of his chest.

## FADET, FARFADET

Fadets are diminutive beings in the folklore of Poitou. They are black and covered with hair and reported to live in underground tunnels, The fadets were seen pulling a strange vehicle with whining wheels in the 1850s near the River Egray.

## FAIRY

An otherworldly being of diminutive or roughly human stature, male or female, generally humanoid in appearance. The word fairy as we have it today stems from inaccurate usage, for fairy or, as it was sometimes spelt, faerie, originally denoted enchantment The original word for a fairy being was 'fay'. *Fairy* has largely usurped the meaning of the last word, but these days, when spelled *faerie*, it is sometimes used with its original significance. Amongst some modern pagan groups the spelling *faerie* seems preferred to that of *fairy*. In Scots the term elf* equates to English fairy.

Our terms fairy and fay go back to the Fates or Parcae of classical mythology. These three deities were called Lachesis, Clotho and Atropos. They were the goddesses of destiny and even Zeus, the chief of the gods, was under their control, as the satirist Lucian makes clear to us. The Fates may have started out in Greece as a single Fate (Moira) who fragmented into three. Lachesis decreed what each man's fate would be, Clotho spun it out for him and Atropos was destiny itself. The thread of life spun out by Clotho would be severed when it was time for the individual to die.

The fays received their name from the Fates. Cognate words in other languages include Italian *fata*, Occitan *fada* and Spanish *hada*. In French the word became *fée*, whence English *fay*. Originally fays were beings of fairy, but by the time of the late Tudors the term fairy had come to mean the being itself.

The term was applied to otherworldly beings of all sizes, many of which may have been worshipped as gods in pagan times. It was applied to Celtic beings such as the Gaelic *Sídh* and the Welsh *Tylwyth Teg*. It should be stressed that many fairies were human in size or even slightly taller. In France they had magic wands, perhaps an echo of the staffs carried by the Fates. Some, such as Morgan Le Fay*, Holda* and Berchte*, would seem to be somewhat (but not greatly) reduced goddesses. Sometimes they may have been thought identical with the dead, as primitive people would not have distinguished readily between other-worldly beings, so that god and ghost would have been confused. Access to the fairy realm seems to have been at times over or through water. Thus the Lady of the Lake of Arthurian romance should not perhaps be thought of so much as living in the lake as using the lake as a portal between earth and the otherworld. Fairy countries such as Tír na nÓg were thought of as lying beyond or even under the sea; for example the Irish Tír fó Thuinn, 'Land Under Wave'. Sometimes fairies were thought of as living underground.

Modern literature, especially picture books for children, has tended to make fairies twee; but to our forebears their society was much like that of humans and they even indulged in fighting. Kirk* tells us that they sustain wounds and live longer than we do, but eventually die or at least pass on to some other state, for they believe that nothing dies really, but, like both sun and year, everything goes in a lesser or greater circle. Kirk also praises their large houses, which he affirms are not usually discernable by "vulgar eyes".

Today the term fairy is used to cover a wide variety of differing beings on which separate articles will be found throughout this volume.

# FAIRY BOY OF LEITH

This individual was no fairy, but rather a mortal who drummed for the fairies. His story is recorded in R. Bovet's *Pandaemonium* (1684), the author having obtained it from a Captain Burton, who claimed he was told by the boy that each Thursday he beat the drum for "a sort of people" who would meet under a great hill between Edinburgh and Leith. He was one of many musicians and often they were taken to France or the Netherlands. He would enter the hill through a pair of gates not normally visible to humans. Within was a habitation containing large rooms.

# FAIRY BAPTISM

In the Isle of Man it used to be said that, sometimes before a baby was born, the fairies would act out a mock baptism of the child, so they would have power over it.

# FAIRY CHIMNEYS

Natural rock towers in Turkey. They are called in Turkish *peri bacalari*, which would indicate they were once thought the habitat of peris*, but these days they are considered the dwelling places of the jinn*.

# FAIRY COWS

A number of tales relate to fairy cows and their help to mankind. In South Lopham (Norfolk) such a cow came and allowed herself to be milked by the people. When the famine ceased she departed, leaving an impression on what came to be called the Ox-foot Stone. A pure white cow of fairy origin did the same service for the famine-struck people of Mitchell's Fold in Shropshire. It was understood that each person was allowed to take only a pailful of milk. When a witch milked the cow into a riddle and thus milked her dry, the cow left. The same treatment actually killed a fairy cow at Stanion in Northamptonshire. Its alleged bone is preserved there. A fairy cow treated in this way which then turned into a monster was killed by the legendary Guy of Warwick. A famous Welsh fairy cow, Y Fuch Frech, was known in Clwyd, where she left her name at Fynnon y Fuch Frech (her well) and Preseby Fuch Frech (her crib). Treated as the others mentioned above she eventually disappeared into a lake. Fairy cows, milk white in colour, were to be found in the region of Llyn Barfog, North Wales. One strayed onto farmland on one occasion and was rescued from butchering by its fairy mistress.

## FAIRY CROSS PLAIN

At this location near Fryup (Yorkshire) fairies were seen in the early 20th Century.

## FAIRY DOG

(Gaelic *cu sith*) A large black dog whose poisonous paw is injurious to all who come in contact with it. If it appears in a locality, all the dogs start howling. It features in Scottish belief.

## FAIRY DOGS

There are various traditions in Wales about fairy dogs which have become lost, were found by humans and at length reclaimed by the fairies.. In one case where the human had used the dog cruelly, he was rewarded, as he thought, with a bag of gold coins, but these turned into leaves.

## FAIRY FLAG

A flag held by the chief of the Clan MacLeod of Dunvegan in Scotland. According to legend, one of the chiefs of the clan married a fairy. She had a son, but subsequently returned to fairyland. She came back to Dunvegan Castle that night and placed a covering of silk around the boy. That night the baby was brought into the hall where a feast was was in progress and fairy voices announced that the covering was a flag, to be waved only in great need: if it were used for a trivial reason, certain specified misfortunes would fall upon the Clan MacLeod. The first two times the flag was raised, the need was indeed great. In the first, the MacLeods were losing a battle, but, when the flag was raised, their fortune turned and they won. In the second, the raising of the flag resulted in the end of a plague which had struck the cattle. But the third time it was waved by a sceptic to show the curse was but a legend without foundation and the misfortunes prophesied fell on the clan. The flag can be seen in Dunvegan Castle today.

# FAIRY FOOD

It is considered unwise to eat fairy food, for, once it is ingested, you will be under the fairies' power. Thus, St Collen declined the food offered him by Gwyn* ap Nudd on Glastonbury Tor. Thomas the Rhymer* sensibly refused an apple offered by the Fairy Queen. Readers of the classics will remember that the reason Persephone had to remain for six months of the year in Hades was because she had eaten six pomegranate seeds while there.

As to the food fairies actually eat, Kirk* speaks of Quintessences and Ethereal Essences, the kind of things that are particularly difficult to obtain in today's fast food restaurants. He speaks also of their appetite for corn and "spiritous liquors". Brownies*, he adds, sometimes bake bread. He says fairies do not eat much, but, when they do, their food is served by pleasant children like enchanted puppets. Lewis Spence tells us fairies like the milk of red deer, goat and cow. The root of the silver weed is consumed by fairies in Scotland.

# FAIRY GODMOTHER

The most well-known fairy godmother is undoubtedly that of Cinderella, but she is not the only one. It may even be the case that in the original version of *Cinderella*, before it was put into its present literary guise by either Charles or Pierre Perrault in 1697, the fairy godmother's role was taken by the ghost of the heroine's dead mother, for, in the corresponding German account, Aschenputtel repairs to a tree growing over her mother's grave, where a white bird (?the mother's soul?) supplies her with her requisites. Tom Thumb* has a fairy godmother while in Countess d'Aulnoy's tale of *Finette*, a fairy godmother advises the heroine.

# FAIRY HERON

This creature was a fairy being in heron form. He was about to be devoured by a sea-serpent when the Maori hero Rata rescued him.

## FAIRY HOUND

This creature was credited with existence in Scotland. Its coat was dark green, its ears greener yet and it was the size of a two-year old cow. It made large tracks. The traveller heard it bark but three times before he was pulled down. It served as watchdog for the fairies.

## FAIRY ISLANDS

In Wales fairies were believed to visit markets at Milford Haven and Laugharne, having come from certain islands. These islands were sometimes descried by humans. They were connected to the land by underground passages.

## FAIRY MARKET

Bovet in his *Pandaemonium* (1684) tells us of a man who, riding by Blackdown (Somerset) saw a fairy market on the hillside. The fairies' stature seems to have been that of ordinary small people, rather than diminutive beings or dwarfs*. They were clad in red, blue or green and wore high crowned hats. Though he could see them as he approached, when he arrived they had become invisible; yet when he rode off somewhat he could see them once again. He was then seized by a pain and suffered lameness the rest of his days. An informant told Ruth L. Tongue that his grandfather had seen the Fairy Market about 1856.

## FAIRY MARRIAGES

Various tales tell of humans marrying fairies. In the case of a woman marrying a fairy man, she sometimes needs the assistance of a human midwife to deliver her child. In tales where a man weds a female fairy, the union often involves a prohibition (such as not touching the fairy with a bridle) which the husband breaks. The fairy then returns home.

## FAIRY PARLOUR

A name give to some of Hangingstones rocks on Ilkley Moor (Yorkshire) where fairies are supposed to live in a hole in a rock.

## FAIRY RING
A circle in the ground where fairies are supposed to dance.

## FAIRY SADDLE
A stone wall on the Isle of Man, which resembles a saddle. The story goes that a clergyman found that a little man in a green jacket was letting his horse loose each night. When the little man saw he was observed by the cleric, he vanished, leaving a saddle, which later turned into stone, on the fence.

## FAIRY TREES
In Ireland trees associated with the fairies are the white-thorn, hazel, blackthorn, bourtree (elder), sally (willow), holly, birch, oak and ash and sometimes the rowan. Juniper and ivy are associated with fairies in Scotland. In Northern Europe belief existed in the elder mother (Hylde-moer) or elder queen (Hylde-vinde) who resided in elder trees.

## FANKENMANNIKIN
A hairy and usually naked diminutive being in Swiss and Austrian folklore. He accompanies the fangg, a kind of female giant.

## FATHER CHRISTMAS
This character started out as the master of ceremonies in the mumming plays of England, which also included such characters as Saucy Jack and a large head upon a pair of legs called Niddy Noddy. There is little doubt that he can be traced to the German god Woden (= Norse Odin), wearing an animal skin inside out, the blood providing the red colour, However, the term 'Father Christmas' is not recorded before the 15th Century. He may be identical with the King of Christmas mentioned as riding at Norwich in 1443 and with the Yule who rode at York in 1572. In Continental Europe, meanwhile, St Nicholas was a gift-giver, but his costume would seem also to go back to Woden. In the United States he was given the name Santa Claus and was renowned in the poem by C.C. Moore entitled *The Night Before Christmas* (1823). In Britain, the two characters were to become fused. In

America Santa Claus is also known as Kris Kringle. This is because in Germany and Austria there is a gift giver known as the *Christkindl* (Christ Child) who was frequently portrayed by a white-robed girl dressed in a veil with her head sporting a star. In Germany the gift-giver was also known as *Schimmelreiter* (white horse rider) which would indicate his connection with his connection with Woden. He was also known as Pelze Nicol and Weihnachtsman. His sleigh is pulled by reindeer in North America and the British Isles. In Australia it is drawn by six white kangaroos.

## FAUN

In Roman mythology, fauns were half man and half goat. They had horns. Readers of English are often familiar with this being because one plays a prominent part in the children's story *The Lion, the Witch and the Wardrobe* (1950) by C.S. Lewis. There was a Roman god called Faunus who was associated with both prophecy and agriculture. He had a female counterpart called Fauna or Faula. The exact relationship of Faunus to fauns generally has given rise to various opinions. One school held that a belief in a species of fauns led eventually to their coalescing into a single god Faunus; another that the god Faunus came first and was later multiplied into numerous fauns (*fauni*).

Some of the folletti* of modern Italian folklore are said to be of faunish descent. Fauns were later identified with the Greek satyrs*, quite distinct creatures in origin. In modern times a Scotsman, R. Ogilvie Crombie, associated with the Findhorn* Foundation, claimed to have encountered a faun in the Royal Botanic Gardens, Edinburgh.

## FEAR DEARG

(Irish, 'red man') A diminutive being in Irish lore, a prankster but a good-natured one. He can make his voice produce a great variety of sounds.

## FENODYREE

A hairy, shaggy being in Manx folklore who helped about the house and threshed corn. There is some doubt as to whether the fenodyree is an individual or a species, according to one account, he is in exile in Man because he absented himself from the Fairy Court at Harvest Moon. (He had been in the company of his beloved). Just as brownies* were supposed to leave in anger if offered clothes, so too was the fenodyree. In one folk tale he was supposed to have taken up residence in Glen Rushen. He was also supposed to be found on farms near Colby and Douglas.

## FERIERS, FERISHERS
Name of fairies in Suffolk, where they were supposed largely to be sandy-coloured. They would not hang around when a person appeared, but you would know you were in a room where feriers had been if you saw stars appear beneath your feet.

## FINDHORN
Place in Scotland where Eileen and Peter Caddy set up a vegetable garden in 1962. They claimed they were assisted by nature spirits, which are called gnomes*, elves* and fairies. Certainly flowers and vegetables grew at an amazing rate on most unpromising ground. The Caddies had as an associate Dorothy Maclean who claimed to be in touch with nature spirits she called devas*. She explained that these devas used energy for materialising the forms in the world while spirits of the gnome and fairy kind used the guidelines and energy with which the devas supplied them. A scholar called R. Ogilvie Crombie, who claimed sightings of various fairy-type beings, acted as ambassador for the Caddys to the nature spirits.

## FINVARRA
(Irish *Fionnbharra*, originally *Fionnbharr*) The King of the Fairies of Connacht, the western province of Ireland. His name may originally have been an adjective (meaning 'white- topped') applied to the hill of Knockmaa in Co Galway, where he resides, later taken to be the name of the fairy king reigning there. Finvarra was often regarded as beneficent to man.

## FINZ-WEIBEL
A wood-wife in Bavarian folklore, said to inhabit the Finz. She is spotted and wears a broad-brimmed hat.

*Fion*

## FION

A type of diminutive being in Breton folklore. The fions' size may be indicated by the fact that their swords are merely the length of pins*.

## FOLLETTO

A term generally applied to sprites in Italy, particularly those descended from silvans*, is folletti. They are magical and generally (but not universally) benevolent, looking and acting like six-year old children.

## FLIBBERTIGIBBET

An evil spirit in the folklore of Norfolk the flibbertigibbet frightened girls at night.

## FREUDIAN INTERPRETATION OF FAIRY TALES

The idea has gained a certain vogue in recent times that many fairy tales can be interpreted in accordance with the theories of Sigmund Freud (1856-1939). Persons advocating this theory would argue that a story such as *Jack and the Beanstalk* illustrates the Oedipus Complex, the giant being Jack's father, whom he kills in order to live happily ever after with his mother.

Such an argument must be treated with caution and cannot be said to have been proven though in the case of the modern fairy play *Peter Pan* (1904) such an interpretation does seem justified as it is obsessed with motherhood and the characters of the children's father and Hook are often portrayed by the same actor.

## FUATH

The fuaths are water-spirits of Scotland. Their feet are webbed and their hair is yellow. Though endowed with manes and tails, they lack noses. They are hairy, except for their faces. Marriage between humans and fuaths is not unknown. The eyes of fuaths are large and round and their garb is green.

## FUDDITU

A Sicilian sprite whose power is lost if his red cap is removed.

## FUJETTU

A kind of mischievous Calabrian sprite who causes trouble in houses occupied by seven families.

# G

### GAHE
See GA'N

### GALLEY-BEGGAR
A being so called appears in Somerset folklore. He would place his head under an arm and go sliding down the hillside on a hurdle. He would laugh wildly.

### GALLITRAP
A term used in somerset to describe a ring, supposedly made by pixies* riding on colts. If you stand in this, you are in the pixies' power, but if you put in a single foot, you may escape.

### GA'N
Subterranean and mountain-dwelling beings in Apache lore, who left the earth because of sickness and death. There is some evidence that they had their origin as fertility spirits. The term *ga'n* is used amongst the White Mountain Apaches. Similar beings are called *gahe* by the Chricahua and Mescalero Apaches.

### GELLO
A kind of female demon in Greek lore. Originally there was a single Gello who, in spectral form, attacked children on the isle of Lesbos. In due course these became a species. They will suck the blood of, or carry off and devour, children.

### GENIE
See JINN

*Giant*

# GHILLE DUBH

A benign mountain spirit in Scottish folklore, reported as dressed in leaves and moss. He will bring home lost children. He was supposedly seen in the Loch a Dring region in the second half of the 18th Century.

# GIALOUT

A fairy in Gueulette's *Chinese Tales* (1723). She rewarded Mammoun for his kindness to her when she was in serpent form by giving him the power of repairing broken objects.

# GIANE

Sardinian sprites, very diminutive in stature. Originally they were five foot females who used to eat humans, giving birth three days later.

# GIANT

Belief in giants is to be found in many cultures, they play an important part in mythology, such as the giants that attacked Olympus or those who fought with Thor. Giants were used to explain natural or man-made features of whose origins the storytellers possessed no clue such as the rock at Duclair on the Seine called the Chair of Gargantua after a famous French giant. The Polynesians believed in giants who had intermarried with humans. The Fijian giant Flaming Teeth was killed by humans but, from the teeth which gave him his name, they obtained fire. Some giants might have been gods in origin, such as the Welsh Yspadadden Penkawr. According to the *Heldenbuch*, God created the giants so they could fight against the dragons and savage beasts of the mountains,, thereby protecting the dwarfs*. When the giants grew in number and wickedness, oppressing the dwarfs, God sent the heroes to aid the latter.

The usual giant of fairy tale is large, lumbering and unintelligent, sometimes with more than one head and well advised to avoid meeting people named Jack. His cry is "Fee fi, for fum'. An early form of this occurs as 'Fy, fa, fum' in Nashe, *Here With You to Saffron Warden* (?1596). Giants were believed to have ruled Britain in ancient times, under their king, Albion. Goemagot, last of these giants, was slain by Corineus, who gave his name to Cornwall.

A list of celebrated giants:-
*Agrius* (Gk. myth) - giant who rebelled against the gods
*Albion* - son of Neptune, slain by Hercules.
*Alcyoneus* - leader of the giants' rebellion against the Greek gods
*Amerant* - killed by Guy of Warwick.
*Angrboda* (Norse) - giantess, mother of monsters by Loki.
*Ascapart* - killed by Bevis of Hampton.
*Atlas* - one of the Titans, placed holding up the sky on his shoulders; turned to stone by Perseus.
*Balan* - a valiant giant from whom Amadis of Gaul rescued Gabrioletta.
*Bell* - Leicestershire giant, famous for the leaps he took on horseback; also the name of a giantess, wife of Wade.
*Balor* - giant with lethal eye, slain by the Celtic god Lugh.
*Bendigeidfran* - Welsh giant who invaded Ireland.
*Bergion* - brother of Albion; ruler of Ireland.
*Blunderbore* - slain by Jack the Giant-Killer.
*Bolster* - Cornish giant who fell in love with St Agnes.
*Colbrand* - Danish giant killed by Bevis of Hampton.
*Cormoran* - killed by Jack the Giant-Killer.
*Coulin* - according to Spenser, a giant who was chased by Debon until he fell into a chasm.
*Dondasch* - in oriental story, servant of Seth son of Adam.
*Ferracute* - killed by Roland (Orlando).
*Finn* - Irish hero, in later lore a giant, built Giant's Causeway.
*Galligantus* - defeated by Jack the Giant-Killer.
*Gargantua* - French giant, associated with megaliths.
*Geirrod* - killed by Thor.
*Giant of St Michael's Mount* - killed by King Arthur.
*Goemagot* (Gogmagog) - British giant, killed by Corineus.
*Holiburn* - Cornish giant.
*Hrungir* - killed by Thor.
*Hymir* - in Norse lore, giant of the sea.
*Idris* - Welsh giant who dwelt on Cader Idris.

*Jack o' Legs* - English giant, reminiscent of Robin Hood, in that he robbed from the rich and gave to the poor.

*Jarnsaxa* - giantess, mother of Magni by the god Thor.

*Leon Gawr* - founder of Chester.

*Luter* - Irish giant with fourteen heads.

*Maelor* - Welsh giant who had sons called Cornipyn, Bwba and Grugyn

*Morgante* - character in Pulci's *Morgante maggiore* (1488).

*Og* - giant in Hebrew lore; Noah saved him from the flood by letting him hold onto a rope ladder.

*Rience* - giant captured by Balin and Balan (Arthurian romance).

*Surt* - in Norse lore, a giant who will bring heaven and earth to a fiery end.

*Thiazi* (Norse) - stole the apples of youth.

*Thrym* - stole Mjollnir, the hammer of Thor.

*Thunderbore* - Cornish giant.

*Trebegean* - giant who lived near Land's End and would pick affrighted sailors off their ships.

*Wade* - giant supposed to have been buried near Whitby; father of Wayland* Smith. He had a boat called Guingelot. On the Continent Wade was also known, and associated with the sea through which he waded (hence his name).

*Xelua* - giant in Aztec legend.

*Ymir* - in Norse mythology a giant in primeval times, brought into being when the cold of the north met the heat of the south. After his death, his body formed the earth. All giants were his descendants.

*Yspadadden* - Welsh giant, whose peculiar eye had to be opened with a fork; father of Olwen.

## GITULIUS

An Old Czech term for a kind of sprite, possibly a homesprite*, as it is glossed kobold*. The word may be of Latin origin coming from Gaetulius, one of the Gaetuli, an African people. If so, we have no clue as to its native name.

*Gnome*

## GLAISTIG

A kind of Scottish fairy, usually, though not exclusively, female. Some of them have the characteristics of a homesprite*, their loyalty being to the house, not to the family which occupies it. They frequent only more prosperous homes. The glaistig is said to be not a fairy in origin, but a human woman who has been made a fairy by magic. A glaistig might look after cattle rather than a a household. Offerings of milk were left out for her. She could show blood-sucking tendencies. Glaistigs have sometimes shown a predeliction for snuff. In appearance the glaistig is short, dressed in green, with her hair reaching to her heels. Male glaistigs seem confined to parts of the Isle of Skye.

## GLASHTYN

A species of goblin* found in the Isle of Man. The glashtyn may have been something like a Scottish kelpie*, changing shape from horse to human and male glashtyns were well known for their powers of attraction to female humans. The distinction between a glashtyn and a fenodyree* is not always clear.

## GLORIANA

In Spenser's unfinished *Faerie Queene* (1590-96), the name of the fairy queen of the title, the daughter of Oberon*. The whole poem is an allegory in which Gloriana represents Elizabeth I and Fairyland stands for England.

## GNOME

From the Latin *gnomus*, a word perhaps coined by Paracelsus (1493-1541), who maintained that gnomes were diminutive creatures that lived in the element of earth and could move through it like a fish through water. In modern times, these creatures are pictured looking much the same as dwarfs*.

## GOATMAN

In the folklore of Prince George's County, Virginia, a creature with the upper parts of a human and the lower parts of a goat, reminiscent of the Greek satyr*.

*Goblins*

# GOBLIN

This word would seem to be related to Greek *kobaloi*, 'evil spirits' and *kobalos*, a knave. This yielded Latin *cobalus*, later developing into French *gobelin*, whence English *goblin*. Ordericus Vitalis (1075-ca. 1142) uses *gobelinus* to mean a certain spirit. in the vicinity of Evreux. The goblin is generally thought of as diminutive, ugly and malevolent. The term, however, can be applied more widely than this.

## GOLDEMAR, KING

Also called Vollmar, he was a celebrated harp-playing home-sprite* in Germany. The human whose house he shared was one Neveling von Hardenberg. He had his own seat at the table and his own stall for his horse. An unfortunate person once tried to make him fall over, so he could espy his footprints. Goldemar cut him up and roasted him, except for the legs, which he boiled. He ate these and left. The roasting spit and (?some of) the roast meat were kept, disappearing in the 17th Century. When T. Keightley wrote his *Fairy Mythology* (1850), the cooking pot was still in the house, built into the kitchen wall.

## GORGON

In classical mythology, there were three gorgons; Medusa, Sthenno and Euryale. Medusa's glance was so awful that she turned you to stone, but she was killed by the hero Perseus. In modern Greek folklore the gorgon is a kind of mermaid*, half woman, half fish. If gorgons see a ship, they will ask the sailors if Alexander the Great still lives. If they reply in the affirmative, a gorgon will strum her lyre, making the sea calm; but if in the negative, she will wreck the ship, either deliberately causing a storm or by going into a fit of sorrow and accidentally causing one. In one story a gorgon's mother is the sea and her father Alexander.

## GORSKA

A Bulgarian mountain fairy.

*Gorgon*

# GOSSAMER

Gossamer drifting in the air in Autumn was thought in Germany to be spun by elves* and dwarfs*. In modern English writing, fairies are often decked in gossamer.

# GRAC'HED COZ

Fairies who appear as little old women in Brittany.

# GRANT

A kind of spirit which looked like a foal, mentioned in the 13th Century by Gervase of Tilbury.

# GREEN CHILDREN

These mysterious children are often said to be fairies who wandered into human lands. Their story, which is placed in the reign of King Stephen (1135-54) is told by William of Newborough (born ca. 1135) and Ralph of Coggeshall (fl. 1207). It says that two green-coloured children, a boy and a girl, were found at Wolf-pits in Sussex, speaking an unknown language. The boy died, but the girl adapted and grew. She said that they came from a country called St Martin's Land, where the sun did not shine. She and the boy had found their way to England through an underground passage.

It has been suggested that, far from being otherworlders, they were merely children living in the forest, the colour of their skins the result of malnutrition and their strange language but a dialect of English unintelligible to their hearers. The 'St Martin's Land' may have been the nearby Fornham St Martin. A variant of this tale which has been circulated has been set in 19th Century Catalonia at a village called Banjos. This story is a hoax, merely an imitation of the English one, and the village of banjos does not exist.

# GREEN LADIES

(French *Dames Vertes*) These forest dwelling beings are generally annoying or downright dangerous to humans, for example, they can lure young men to their doom.

*Green Man*

# GREEN MAN

Carvings of green men, their hair and beards made of leaves, are often found in churches. By some they are supposed to be of pagan origin, representing fertility spirits. However. this interpretation is by no means certain.

# GREMLIN

The gremlin is a being of modern folklore, supposed to cause mechanical hiccups in aeroplanes. Some have suggested they have always been in existence, but only with the age of aviation have we come to know about them. They are usually mischievous, but occasionally helpful. Some say they have horns, others that they have large ears. In colour they are green or blue/grey. Recent films have depicted them as little furry creatures.

# GRENDEL

An ogre[*]-like monster in the Anglo-Saxon poem *Beowulf*, composed about the 8th Century. He lived out in the moors in a lake with his monstrous mother and was in the habit of killing humans until Beowulf killed him. Grendel had been raiding Heorot, the hall constructed by Hrothgar, King of the Danes, and it was at the latter's hest that Beowulf confronted him. The hero grabbed Grendel and wrenched off his clawed arm, whereupon Grendel, with a deadly wound had to flee. His monstrous mother sought vengeance. She attacked the hall, killing King Hrothgar's much-loved counsellor Aeschere and retrieving her son's arm. Beowulf pursued her and slew her after a fierce struggle on the bottom of the lake where she lived. He found Grendel's body there. He cut off the head and brought it back to Heorot.

# GREY MAN

(Irish *fear liath*) This being appears to be a personification of the fog as which he appears.

# GRUAGACH

Creatures so called appear in the folklore of both Ireland and Scotland. The term, however, is used to denote various types. In

*Gryla*

Ireland it can mean a giant*, ogre*, wizard, goblin* or even, in Co Louth, a champion warrior. (In the last-mentioned area Gruagach was actually given as a personal name to boys). In Scotland the gruagach was often, though not exclusively, female. Whether male or female in Scotland, the gruagach was noted for its long hair. It seems to have some element of divinity about it, for on Skye there were small altars to gruagachs where offerings were left. Elsewhere, gruagachs who looked after cattle were given payments of milk, which one neglected to provide at one's peril, lest the cows be allowed into the corn by the unpaid gruagach. A second failure to pay could lead to the best cow's death. How did the gruagach have so many shapes? The word is possibly derived from Irish *gruaig* (hair) and if so would signify 'the hairy one'. It may originally have meant a kind of hairy wild man, but in due course the word came to be applied to a variety of otherworldly beings. W. G. Wood-Martin opined that it may preserve a memory of the time when the woolly mammoth walked in Ireland.

## GRYLA
Grylas are beings in the folklore of the Faeroes. Mountain dwellers, they have shaggy bodies like sheep, but they walk standing upright. They are dangerous and are used by parents to frighten children. A verse describes one as having forty tails and carrying a sword.

## GUBICH
A forest demon in German lore.

## GUGWES
Gigantic beings in the folklore of the Micmac Indians of Canada. They have faces like bears and have also been compared to baboons. Another name for the gugwes is the *djenu*.

## GUNNA
In the gunna we have an exile from Faerie, living alone, perhaps helping to look after the cattle. In one tale, he vanished when offered clothing, just as the brownie* was wont to do. Found in the Scottish Highlands, he often wears fox- skins.

## GWYLLION

These hag-fairies are to be encountered on lonely Welsh roads. They lead travellers astray. They would sometimes visit houses, where iron implements were concealed from them. This type of creature sometimes coalesced into a single individual called the Old Woman of the Roads.

## GWYN AP NUDD

In Welsh folk belief, the King of the Fairies. He has some of the characteristics of a hunter. In the Arthurian romance of *Culhwch and Olwen* we are told that every year Gwyn fought with Gwythr and whichever of them proved the victor on Doomsday would be given the maiden Creiddylad. This combat indicates that in origin Gwyn was a Celtic divinity and this is reinforced by the fact that his father Nudd is to be identified with the god Nodens. One story says that Gwyn summoned St Collen to meet him at the top of Glastonbury Tor. The saint did so. He refused to eat Gwyn's food and doused him and his followers with holy water, so that they disappeared.

## GWRACH Y RHIBYN

A Welsh hag who appears at cross-roads or on the sides of mountains. Sometimes this being is male.

## GWRAGGED ANNWN

Female fairies of Welsh tradition. They are to be found in lakes and streams.

## GYRE-CARLIN

An important figure in the fairy lore of Scotland. Her name would seem to be derived from a word meaning 'witch', but her functions would have been very much those of a fairy queen. Known by the name of Nicnevin (? Gaelic *nic neamhan*, 'daughter of heaven), she rode the storm. She appeared to be an old woman, much skilled in spinning and bringing with her a small child which she bathed before going to bed. She could confer the gift of swift spinning.

# H

## HAHNEN, FRAU VON

The protagonist of a Czech fairy tale. She acted as midwife* to a water nix* and was given three pieces of gold as payment. She was told to keep them in the family, but, when her daughter-in-law gave them away, their fortunes declined.

## HÄRDMANDLE

The dwarfish hillmen of Swiss folklore. They are of a benevolent nature and will drive home stray animals. Their domestic animal is the chamois: they make cheese from its milk. This cheese is magical. If they give you some, each time you bite it, it will replenish itself, but you should not eat it all, or it is gone for good.

## HARLEQUIN

A magical being formerly to be seen in the Harlequinade on the English stage. He had a black mask and a costume spangled with diamonds. He was equipped with a magic slapstick or wand. In due course a fairy tale was enacted before the Harlequinade and this became the Christmas pantomime. The Harlequinade told of how Harlequin became enamoured of Columbine, to the chagrin of Pantaloon.

Harlequin first appeared on the English stage in the 18th Century. His origin was in the Italian Commedia dell'Arte, where he was first found as a comic servant, but later appeared as a more serious character. It is thought he was derived from a being in folklore called Hellekin, leader of the Wild Hunt*

## HART, MR

A schoolmaster who taught John Aubrey and told that celebrated antiquary that in the year 1633-4 once near nightfall he saw

*Hedley Kow*

circles in the grass, where he saw a great many fairies dancing, nor could he leave the spot, much as he wished to. He then fell and they pinched him all over, then leaving. He was still lying there in the morning.

## HEARTH

In English lore, fairies would dance here. In the old days, before the invention of television, the hearth would have been the focal point of the home which indicates that the fairies associated with it may have been household gods in origin.

## HEDLEY KOW

A kow i.e. spirit, that frequented Hedley on the Hill (Northumberland). It would appear in any of a number of guises, such as a donkey, a cow or a wisp of straw. It was of a prankish disposition and was known to cause chaos in the kitchen. A well-known story depicts it as a piece of straw. An old woman picks it up and cannot understand why it keeps growing heavier. She puts it down, perplexed, where upon it jumps up and runs off.

## HEIMCHEN

Beings of an elfin type in Berchte's* train.

## HEIZEMÄNN

A homesprite, in the region of Cologne.

## HERLA

In English legend, an ancient British king who visited the fairies. When the visit was completed, the fairy king gave him a little hound and, as he and his entourage set out for home, his host warned him and his men not to alight from their steeds until the hound jumped groundwards. On returning, they met a man who could understand them only with difficulty and they learned that, instead of being away a mere three days as they had thought, they had been absent in Faerie for two centuries. Alarmed by this, some of the men dismounted and turned to dust. The others, led by Herla, stayed horsed and rode about for generations. In 1154 Henry II became king and in that year

Herla and his men were seen to plunge into the Wye. There is a probable connection between the legend of Herla and the tradition of the Wild Hunt*

## HERNE THE HUNTER

This being is first mentioned by Shakespeare (*Merry Wives of Windsor*) where it says that Herne with "ragged horns" walks round the oak at midnight every winter. The detail of the antlers has made people speculate that Herne may be in origin a horned god. Shakespeare said he was once a keeper in the park and one Samuel Ireland that he had been a suicide, but these statements need not rule out the possibility that at some remote period Herne was a pagan divinity. The historical novelist W. Harrison Ainsworth in *Windsor Castle* (1843) made him the leader of the Wild Hunt*. A number of appearances of Herne have been alleged in modern times.

## HIBLA-BASHI

A kind of satyr*, half man and half goat, with vampiric tendencies, in the folklore of Iraq.

## HOB

A type of local spirit found in the north of England. Hobs are often troublesome, but they can be helpful at times. They guard stretches of road and moors. See also hobthrust*

## HOBBIT

A fictitious form of faerie being invented by J.R.R. Tolkien, first appearing in *The Hobbit* (1937) and subsequently in the epic *The Lord of the Rings* (1954-5). Hobbits are of diminutive stature and longer lived than humans. They go barefoot, having hairy feet. They call themselves *kuduk*, a word meaning something like 'hole-dweller', as they live in elaborate holes.

## HOBGOBLIN

A sprite in English folklore who often frequents dairies. It is also said they guard treasure and cut wood. Like the brownie", the hobgoblin does not like being offered new clothes. Hobgoblins are hirsute beings, on the uncouth side. Bunyan seems to regard the hobgoblin as an evil being, as he couples it with the fiend.

## HOBTHRUST

A being bearing strong similarities to Robin Goodfellow*. He shows brownie* characteristics, such as working about the house and, like the brownie, he can vanish if offered a payment in clothing. The name Hob Thrust, or Hob Thrush was given to a particular being who was supposed to live in Hob Hurst's House, a barrow at Beeley (Derbyshire). Under the name of Hob Thrush he is, in one folktale, noted for helping an indigent shoemaker by making shoes for him. A particular Hobthrush Hob was to be found in a cave at Mulgrave Woods (Yorkshire). In Yorkshire the terms *hob* and *hobthrush* tend to be used interchangeably, but J. Westwood feels they may once have been distinct, hob being a domestic sprite and hobthrush an outdoor one.

## HÖGFOLK

Beings in Scandinavian folklore living in hills. By nature they are some way between elves* and humans. They look like handsome humans when they appear.

## HOLDA, FRAU

A supernatural being in German folklore, probably originally a goddess, reduced to a sort of fairy being in Christian times. She is generally regarded as beautiful and beneficent, though she can be angered by ill-run households. Snow was attributed to her making her bed in the sky. She would at times frequent the water. Between Christmas and Twelfth Day, a supernatural time in German lore, she would ride about in a wagon. This is reminiscent of the wagon used to carry about the ancient German goddess Nerthus, mentioned by Tacitus. Holda was also a rider of the winds, terrible of aspect, and she was sometimes represented as a hag. Sometimes the Germans called witches' rides Holle-rides. She was connected with spinning. A.s to her origin, she may be the mythological sorceress Hulda, mother by Odin of Thorgerdr and Irpa, two goddesses, who is found in Icelandic saga.

# HOMESPRITE
A general term for beings of the brownie* kind, who care for the home when its denizens are abed.

# HOOPER, HOOTER
A sea-spirit which turns up in the form of a fog at Sennen Cove, Cornwall. Its appearance warned sailors not to go to sea. Once a skipper defied the Hooper and sailed into the fog. Neither he nor his crew was seen again.

# HOP O' MY THUMB
A diminutive fairy being in nursery lore, called by the French Petit Poucet.

# HORSE AND HATTOCK!
A cry, first recorded by John Aubrey in his *Miscellanies* (1696), used by fairies to make themselves fly through the air.

# HOTEI
A gift giver analogous to Father Christmas* in Japanese lore who distributes presents to children except to bad ones, whose misdeeds he can detect with eyes in the back of his head.

# HSIEN
In Chinese folklore, a term generally applied to spirits of the fairy kind. Notable among them are the Pa Hsien (Eight Immortals or Fairies), a group of historical and legendary beings inhabiting a paradisal realm.

# HULDRE-FOLK
A name for sprites in Norway. The male is called huldre-kall, the female hulder. The term is not confined to Norway, for it is found as Faeroese *huldefolk*, Icelandic *huldufolk*. Their music is called *Huldraslaat*. In Old Norse saga, Hulda is the queen of dwarfs" and possibly gave the huldre-folk their name. She in turn is probably a form of the German Holda* .

## HUMPTY DUMPTY

The egg-man of English nursery rhyme. His counterparts are found all over Europe, e.g., German *Giaele-Gaaele*. Swedish *Thille-lille*, etc. His origin is unknown. obscure. The nursery rhyme has not been discovered earlier than about the beginning of the 19th Century.

## HUGON

King Hugon was an ogre* in French nursery lore.

## HUON OF BORDEAUX

The hero of a French romance who inherited the fairy kingdom of Oberon*. His inheritance was put at risk in a later romance when it was found that his wife, Esclarmonde, was a mortal but Jesus changed her into a fairy.

## HYENA MAN

In Mali there is a belief in spirits who, whatever their true form, can turn themselves into a man or a hyena at will.

# I

### IELE

A fairy race in Romanian folklore. The term means 'they' and is a euphemism. They are also called *dinsele*, 'they themselves'. The Iele are sometimes controlled by the human lovers they acquire. They are connected with fertility. They are seen in a cart or with a plough. They enjoy making people sick.

### IHK'AL

Fairy like beings of diminutive stature believed in by the Tzeltal Indians of Mexico. They are covered in hair and they have rockets on their backs which they use to make themselves fly.

### ILEANA

A Romanian fairy who awakens during the night and brings in the day. She has eyes like the sun.

### INCUBUS

A spirit which makes love to women. The father of Merlin was an incubus. The word comes from Latin *incubo*, 'nightmare' and the incubus was originally the nightmare personified. The word is also connected with Latin *incubare*, 'to lie on'. Incubus symptoms may result from sleep paralysis, which occurs in the state between waking and sleeping. Those who experience this usually feel as if there is something heavy on their chests, This accompanies an inability to move or speak. Sleep paralysis is by no means uncommon. The female equivalent of an incubus is called a succubus or succuba. In modern Italian lore, incubi are offspring of matings between male and female fauns*. They hang about the herds, giving them nightmares.

# IRON

Iron is regarded as being a protection against beings of the fairy kind. This has led some to see in fairies a reminiscence of a people unacquainted with iron, defeated in prehistoric times by invaders with iron weapons.

# J

## JACK-IN-THE-GREEN
A character seen in processions represented by a boy covered in greenery. It has been thought that Jack was a folklore character in origin, perhaps having a connection with fertility. However, such a conclusion is premature, as Jack is first recorded in chimney sweeps' processions. There were no chimney sweeps before the 17th Century, so Jack may have been invented by them, but he may have been taken by them from existing folklore.

## JALPARI
A water fairy in Punjabi lore. She has a tendency to try to seduce young men whom she captures and, if they rebuff her, she kills them.

## JASHTESMÉ
Nymphs* in Albanian folklore.

## JEFFRIES, ANNE
She lived in Cornwall and, in 1645, when she was nineteen, she claimed she met six fairies, who offered her fairy food. She said she was at times carried through the air by the fairies and once even taken to Fairyland. A fairy man there became her lover and jealous fairies brought her home. They taught her the healing arts which she used on her fellow humans.

## JENNY GREENTEETH
An evil water-spirit who lived under weeds. She had green teeth and would capture unwary children.

## JERSEY DEVIL

A strange being said to haunt the Pine Barrens of New Jersey. There are varying descriptions of this being, but it is generally depicted as something like a kangaroo with leathery wings and it sometimes has a forked tail. Stories about it circulated in the 19th Century, when it was blamed for many farming disasters. It was supposedly born to a Mrs Leeds who was tired of having children so she wished her next child would be a devil.

In another tradition its mother was a Mrs Shourds. There was a great spate of reported sightings in the year 1909. A taxi driver claimed to have seen it in 1927. There were a number of reports in or around Gibbstown in 1951. Hunt Brothers Circus offered a reward of $100,000 for the creature in 1960. In 1966 locals thought the wholesale destruction of birds and animals on a farm was the Jersey Devil's work.

## JINN

(The proper singular of this word is *jinnee*, anglicised *genie*, from Arabic *jinni*.) Jinn are spirits in Arabian folklore, some good, some bad, longer lived than men, but they will die before the final resurrection. A female jinnee is called a jinneeyeh (Arabic *jinniyeh*). They were formed from fire without smoke, thousands of years before Adam and were ruled by a succession of rulers named Suliman. Readers of *The Arabian Nights* will remember that Aladdin met two of them. In Islamic belief a man may marry a jinnee (though this is not recommended), but a woman may not wed a jinnee. The offspring of a union between the two races is believed to have the attributes of both. A variety of jinn is called the ifrit. This type is generally thought of as evil. With the spread of Islam, belief in jinn spread also. Malaysians believe they can possess people and that there is a King of the Black Jinn called Data Jinn Hitam. In North Africa jinn are thought to have been created from the simoom and it is believed the first jinn was called Asoom Jan Tanushi or Taranushi.

## JOINT-EATER

Kirk* testifies that the explanation for why certain people eat a great deal and yet remain unfattened this is because they have a fairy joint-eater who feeds on the "pith and quintessence" of what the man eats.

## JOLA SVEINAR
The Icelandic equivalent of the Swedish Jultomte*.

## JONES, EDWARD
In *Bye-Gones*, a periodical published from 1871-1939, the following story is related of one Edward Jones, who was the ultimate source of the tale and who vouched for its truth. In the issue of November 14th, 1887, we are told that he accidentally came upon a troop of fairies. Wishing to be rid of him, they asked him whether he would like to be carried off by a high, middle or low wind. He made his choice - we are not told which - and he was then blown through the air by wind and set down many miles away.

## JUDY
A nymph* in the folklore of Bulgaria and Macedonia. She inhabits the water.

## JULBUK
A horned sprite in Scandinavian lore. As his name ('Yule- buck') would imply, he visits the house around Christmas, but in summer and autumn he lives in the woods and fields respectively.

## JULENISSE
The Norwegian and Danish equivalent of the Swedish Jultomte*.

## JULTOMTE
A small being who delivers Christmas gifts in Swedish lore. He is the ruler of the Little People.

# K

## KACHINA

Kachinas are supernatural beings believed in and culted by the Hopi Indians. They are beneficial and of many varieties e.g., gigantic, long-haired, etc. Many of the cultural aspects of Hopi life are said to have been taught them by the kachinas.

## KAF

The legendary range of mountains, inhabited by the Arabian jinn* or the Iranian peris*.

## KAHUI-A-TIPUA

A strange race of beings believed in by the Maori. Some said that they had faces like dogs, some that they were maero*.

## KAKAMORA, KAKANGORA

Diminutive beings in the folklore of the Solomon Islands. Though strong, they do not normally present a threat to mankind, but will occasionally kill and devour a human. A king and queen rule them. They are called kakamora on Guadalcanal, kakanaora on San Cristoval

## KALKADOON

Kalkadoons were giants who, according to Australian aboriginal lore, lived in the Dreamtime.

## KAPPA

In Japanese lore, kappas were strange beings whose webbed hands boasted claws at the end of them. They are supposed to have been seen in Japan from the 9th to the 11th Centuries. They were believed to teach bonesetting and to travel on cucumbers, which they also ate with great delight. Their noses resembled trunks and appeared to be attached to something on

ey were supposed to be found near Kyushu on
 ⅃ and near the Kawacki River. Although
 ⌐ no longer around, it has been suggested that some
 ⌐ₓrn reports of strange creatures refer to kappas.

## KATZENVEIT
A forest demon in German lore.

## KAUKAS
A diminutive homesprite* in Lithuanian lore.

## KEELY, JOHN
According to a report in the Dublin *Irish Press* in 1938, this was
the name of a boy who encountered fairies in Co Limerick. The
first time he saw a single one. The second time he talked with
the fairy. On the following day, witnessed by men hiding in the
bushes, he met two fairies. They had faces like men, hard and
hairy, and were about two feet in height. Noticing the onlookers,
the fairies fled. They were chased but they managed to escape,
staying clean even when they went through hedges.

## KELPIE
A water spirit in Scottish lore. It generally appears as a black
horse. It could appear as a handsome youth, but would be
betrayed by the watercress in its hair. The kelpie's equine form
may be due to suggestion: a Highlander who noticed a strange
grey horse in his herd, saw, by continuing to look at him, that he
was an old man, grey of hair and beard. When a kelpie was tired
of running along a riverbank, it would strike the water with its
tail three times, then disappear. You could catch a kelpie in
horse form if you put over its head a bridle on which the Sign of
the Cross had been made. He could then be made to do work.

## KENSINGTON GARDENS
A park in London, long associated with faerie, for it was here
that J.M. Barrie set the early adventures of Peter Pan*, whose
statue is now to be found there. However, the park had much
earlier fairy associations It was the scene of Thomas Tickell's

poem *Kensington Garden* (1722), which relates that Kennar, a daughter of the fairy king Oberon*, was beloved by Albion, who had been brought to Kensington as a child by the fairy Mikah. Oberon was opposed to their union and expelled Albion, making Kenna marry one Azuriel. Albion obtained the support of Neptune who sent him to Kensington with an army under the command of Oriel, a fairy who ruled a Thames-side realm. Albion fell in the ensuing fracas and Neptune, in retaliation, destroyed Oberon's kingdom. Kenna turned the dead Albion into a snowdrop, using the juice of moly.

## KESHALYI
The good fairies of Romany Gypsy lore. As a result of the king of the demons giving their queen a divorce, every woman of the Keshalyi has to be handed over to the demons at the age of 999 years. The word keshalyi seems to be connected with Romany *kachli*, a spindle.

## KIRATA
A sort of supernatural forest creature in Indian belief. The females are said, at least sometimes, to be golden-hued nymphs* with a propensity towards seducing the virtuous. The males are said by some to be half man, half tiger, the upper half being the tigrine portion.

## KIRK, ROBERT
(1644-92) Scottish Presbyterian minister, wrote a treatise on fairies called *The Secret Commonwealth of Elves, fauns and fairies* (1691). He felt fairies were beings in a state intermediary between men and angels. He died on Doon Hill, which had fairy connections, but, according to legend, he was spirited away by the fairies and an imitation corpse was left in his place. A further tale said that, after his death, he appeared to a doctor, telling him that he was not dead but in Faerie and to tell his cousin Duchray that, at the baptism of his posthumous daughter, he would appear in the room and if he (Duchray) threw the knife he held over his head, Kirk would be released into human society. The doctor dithered about delivering the message and Kirk appeared to him again, telling the physician he would haunt him

*Knecht Ruprecht*

until he complied with his request. The doctor did as he had been bidden. Duchray saw Kirk enter the room at the time of the baptism, but did not throw the knife and Kirk remained in Faerie.

## KIRK ANDREAS

A place on the Isle of Man, the scene of an abduction by fairies. The man carried off spent four years in their realm, but could see what the humans were doing at home, though they could not see him. He could not describe how he had been returned to human society, but thought that he had been perhaps rendered unconscious and then had awoken in the human world.

## KIRNIS

A kind of demon believed in by the Lithuanians. He guards the cherry tree.

## KISIMBI

(plural *bisimbi*) A kind of water nymph* in the folklore of the Congo.

## KLWAKWE

A kind of man-eating giant* in the folklore of the Penobscot Indians of Maine.

## KLAUBAUF

A kind of German sprite with horns and a long beard. His nose and fingers are also long.

## KLAUBAUTERMAN

In Teutonic lore, a kind of sprite found on board ship; also called *kluterman*, *kalfater*.

## KNECHT RUPRECHT

This being, in German lore, wears furs, straws or shaggy raiment. He carries a staff, the Klapperboch, with a wooden goat's head on top. At Christmas, Knecht Ruprecht would appear, sometimes alone, but sometimes with the Infant Jesus or

*Knocker*

Berchte*. While the divine being gave out gifts, Knecht Ruprecht threatened to deal out punishments J. Grimm considers him to be a German equivalent of Robin Goodfellow*. In comedies of the 16th/17th Centuries, he is called *Rüpel, Rüppel*, a cheerful fool.

## KNOCKER

A diminutive being in Cornish folklore. Knockers inhabit mines. Sometimes they will show miners a good place to dig. Sometimes a miner will hear his strikes repeated by a knocker. An alternative name for a knocker is a bucca. In the United States, the term tommyknocker is used for a ghost in a mine.

## KOBOLD

Kobolds are diminutive beings in German folklore. The term is first found in the 13th Century as Latin *coboldus*. They appear to have at first been wooden objects, perhaps household gods, which jugglers brought from under their cloaks. They may have been carved from boxwood and depicted with their mouths open laughing, as there was an expression "to laugh like a kobold". To speak like a kobold meant to speak quietly.

The kobold is a homesprite*. When deciding if he will take up residence in a house he will dirty its milk vessels and bring sawdust and chips of wood inside. If the former are cleaned and the latter not strewn about, he will take up residence.

## KODIN-HALTIA

A house fairy in Finnish lore.

## KOPUWAI

A horrid ogre*, perhaps a maero*, in the belief of the Maoris. He had a dog's head and a pack of two-headed dogs with which he hunted down humans to form his grisly banquets. His name means 'water stomach' from his capacity to imbibe large quantities of water. He was eventually killed by Maoris who started a fire outside the entrance to his cave and, when he sought to escape through a hole in the roof, battered him to death.

## KORRIGAN
Alternative spelling of corrigan*.

## KRATTI
A Finnish spirit, guardian of property.

## KRSASPA
An Iranian epic hero, he at length did not die, but fell into a sleep. 99,999 fairies provided a guard for him.

## KUCDA-QA
A kind of spirit in the belief of the Tlingit Indians. Originally, it was possibly thought to have been the spirit of a man who had drowned or died in the woodlands. It was called a 'land otter man'.

## KUNAL-TROW
A melancholic kind of trow*. No females of this species exist, so our kunal-trow must marry a human, who will die giving birth. Until the son of such a union attains his majority, the kunal-trow cannot die.

# L

## LAMIA

In classical mythology, Lamia was the mother of certain children of Zeus whom the jealous Hera slew, so she developed a twisted nature, killing the children of other mothers. Sometimes lamias were spoken of in the plural and were said to seduce and then destroy their lovers. In modern Greek folklore lamias look like women of large stature and uncouth appearance. Their feet may be hooves or made out of bronze. They may have more than two. They have a bloodlust and are generally hungry, dirty and of low intelligence. They like to eat newly born babies. Generally a lamia's husband is a dragon and perhaps a disgruntled dragon as lamias make very poor housekeepers.

## LAMIA OF THE SEA

A being in Greek folklore, perhaps identical with the Queen of the Shore. Her singing voice is pleasant. She dances on the waves and causes waterspouts and whirlwinds, which are perhaps her vehicles.

## LAMIÑAK

A kind of fairy in Basque lore. Lamiñaks issue instructions to humans, but confusingly say the opposite to what they mean. They are lucky and insist on cleanliness. Their usual dwellings are subterranean. They will sometimes enter a human's house by the chimney. They have been known to leave changelings*.

## LANE, LOUGH

A small lake in Westmeath (Ireland). A strange tale, purportedly true, is told about it in an issue of the *Irish Fireside* (7th January, 1884). The events in the tale, we are told, took place in 1869. A boy had been stolen by the fairies and apparently taken into the lough and a fairy left in his place. The parish priest managed to have the boy returned for long enough to say how he could be retrieved permanently. When this information was divulged, the boy was again replaced by the fairy. The latter was then dipped three times in the waters of the lough and the boy emerged and walked over the water to his father. On the way home, they were escorted by fairy soldiers who had come out of the lake. The boy's mother was not supposed to speak to him on the way home, but she did, so he had to be returned to the lake. The whole operation had to be repeated, but this time it was successful and the boy restored to his home.

## LA PLATA DWARFS

These beings of a faerie-like nature were reportedly seen in the city of La Plata, Argentina, in 1983. They were described as 'green'. Sightings occurred near an abandoned house and it was said the beings had come from a well in the grounds. One witness described a being he saw as having skin like a reptile and one eye. Another said they looked like wrinkled old men and that, when he had fallen running away from them, one of them had thrown a brick at him.

## LAURIN

A dwarf* king in the *Heldenbuch* who was overcome by the hero Dietrich. As a result of his further underhandedness he was taken to Bekne, where he became a clown. He had married a human maiden whom he had abducted.

## LAURU

A small sprite in Italian folklore. He tries to seduce women. If he is unsuccessful, he will give the woman concerned nightmares until she hangs the horns of a bull or a ram over the door.

## LAZY LAWRENCE

A spirit in Somerset and Hampshire associated with horses. He sometimes takes the form of a pony.

## LEANNÁN SÍ

A fairy lover in Irish lore. Desire for her consumes her innamorato, but it is only by passing through the portals of death that he can obtain her.

## LEPRECHAUN

A diminutive being in Irish folklore. The word comes from Irish *lughchorpán*, 'little body'. Irish forms of the name include *leipreachán, lúracán, lúchramán, lurgadán*. The earliest English form recorded is *lubrican*, which exists in a number of 17th Century works. Generally the leprechaun is depicted as a solitary fairy, a shoemaker, known to possess a crock of gold. However, in the story of Fergus Mac Léide we meet a whole leprechaun society, with a king and a queen, who become captives of the Ulstermen.

## LESHY

A Slavic forest spirit, he rules the woodlands, sleeping in abandoned huts. He can alter his size. The leshy has only one eye, which is not endowed with brow or lashes. He has horns and the feet of a goat. Green hair grows all over him; the skin underneath it is grey. Leshies sometimes live in fields. They hibernate. Leshy fights cause storms. For using the forest for grazing animals, men must make offerings to the leshies. Leshies can be hostile, leading men astray in the woods or even, like. the rusalkas*, tickling them to death.

## LILE HOB

A hob* who lived on the road at Blea Moor (Yorkshire). He would jump onto passing carts.

## LIPSIPSIP

Diminutive spirits in the folklore of Vanuatu.

## LISUNKA

The female of the leshy*.

## LITTLE MEN IN CARS

In *Modern Mysteries of Britain* (1987) Janet and Colin Bord report an incident at Wollaton Park, Nottingham, which took place in 1979. A group of four children described seeing little men with white beards and wrinkled features driving cars resembling bubble-cars in the area of soft ground near the lake. Their appearance was heralded by the sound of a bell. They wore caps with bobbles.

## LITTLE RED MEN

A race of diminutive beings in the folklore of Tennessee. They are supposed to dwell in the woods near the Mississippi. A race of tree climbers, they are said to wear cast-off clothes abandoned by humans. In size, they roughly equal a ten-year old child.

## LITTLE SPIRITS

Dwarfish spirits in the folklore of the Sioux. They live on a mountain near the Whitestone River, are about $1\frac{1}{2}'$ tall and shoot arrows at humans who enter their territory.

## LOIREAG

A diminutive female sprite in Scottish lore. She is concerned with the making and fulling of cloth.

## LOLOK

Diminutive beings in the folklore of the Minahadsa of Indonesia.

## LONDONDERRY AIR

An Irish tune, the unofficial anthem of Northern Ireland. It is supposed to have been learned from the fairies. It was collected by Jane Ross and printed in the Petrie collection (1855). Various words have been put to it, the most well-known by F.E. Weatherly.

## LORELEI

A water nymph* of the Rhine, who would sit on her rock and lure sailors to their deaths. When a party of soldiers led by one

Diether came to overcome her, she called on the Rhine, her father, to provide her with steeds. A storm arose sending up foamy waves resembling mounts onto the rocks and these she followed as though in a chariot drawn by them into the river. When she went beneath the waves, the storm subsided.

A euhemerised version of the tale makes her a damsel of Bacharach whose lover had gone to the wars and not returned. While she waited for him, huge numbers of young men fell in love with her, but she would accept none of them. She was accused of using sorcerous powers to obtain their affections, but was acquitted of this when tried. The Archbishop of Cologne gave her permission to stay at a convent, where she might garner peace from young suitors. On the way there she stood on a rock and saw the ship bearing her true love returning. It foundered on the rocks and she, seeing his plight, jumped into the water to join him and they were united in death.

## LUOT-CHOZJIK
A female spirit who, according to the Lapps, is the protectress of their reindeer when they are allowed to wander untended in the summer.

## LURLINE
The opera *Lurline* (1860) by Wallace owes something to the legend of Lorelei*. Lurline was a nymph of the Rhine, daughter of King Rhineberg. She fell in love with Rudolph, a human, and gave him a magic ring which enabled him to dive into the river and find her. After a time he came ashore once more, the ring was stolen and he forgot her. At length she won him back and they were reunited in her watery abode.

## LUTIN
The lutin features in Norman and Breton folklore. The word is found in Old French as both *neiton* and *luitun*. The meaning of its name is obscure: it may indicate smallness or or nocturnal habits. Lutins are diminutive beings dressed in green. They can take on the shape of any animals. Activity of the poltergeist variety is attributed to them. They are seen, it is said, at

crossroads and will attack night time wayfarers. They sometimes help humans around the house, but are just as likely to cause them annoyance. They greatly like horses and children and give warning of disasters. A way of driving them off is to sprinkle flax on the floor. In Brittany confusion exists between lutins and corrigans*.

# M

## MAB

A queen of the fairies mentioned by Shakespeare in *Romeo and Juliet* (?1595). She is also called queen of the fairies by the poets Drayton and Herrick and is described as "mistress-fairy" in Ben Jonson's *Entertainment at Althorpe* (1603). She seems to be a character drawn from genuine folklore rather than a literary creation. One of her duties seems to have been to act as the fairies' midwife. A connection with the Irish Queen Maeve (herself probably a goddess in origin) has been postulated, but this suggestion must be treated with caution.

## MAERO

A kind of supernatural race, believed in by the Maoris, who were said to have been the first inhabitants of New Zealand, whom the Maoris defeated. The Eyre Mountains and Bayonet Reefs were supposed to be the habitats of the maero. They were regarded as hairy and having nails long enough to spear birds and fish. One kind, the Maeroero-repuwai had good-looking women and were a tall race.

## MAJAHALDJAS

The homesprite* of Estonian folklore, also called the koduhaldjas. Food and drink are left out for him.

## MALEKIN

A child taken by the fairies, according to Ralph of Coggeshall (fl. 1207). She was to be found at Dagworth Castle, Suffolk, where she resided invisibly. She could talk both English and Latin. She appeared once to a servant girl, at the latter's request. She looked like a small child in a white tunic.

## MAMUCCA

This diminutive being in Italian folklore likes to hide things in a house. There is general uproar when the article is discovered to be missing. Afterwards, the mamucca appear with the missing item and a splitting grin. The mamucca dresses like a monk.

## MAIMUNE

A fairy in the Arabian Nights. Cameralzanan, son of the Sultan Shahzamar, was noted for his beauty. Badoura daughter of Emperor Gaiour of China, was the world's most beautiful woman and, when she was asleep, she was brought into Cameralzanan's bed-chamber, that he might behold her. Unfortunately, he was fast asleep on her arrival. The fairy Maimune took this opportunity to bite him on the neck. He awoke, saw Badoura and subsequently married her.

## MAN IN THE MOON

That the moon was believed to have a solitary inhabitant is attested by the nursery rhyme which claims he made a voyage to earth and sought the way to Norwich, perhaps a curious destination for an interplanetary traveller. According to German belief, the Man in the Moon was placed there because he gathered faggots on the Sabbath or else strewed brambles in the way of those bound for Mass. He may be accompanied by a woman, whose offence was to make butter on a Sunday. Sometimes folklore gives him a dog. In Scandinavian belief the moon stole two children who were gathering water. Their names were Hjuki and Bil and they could be seen from earth as the markings on the moon. These two, according to S. Baring-Gould, are the originals of jack and Jill, whose hill climbing technique left so much to be desired. There is an old Somerset song called *The man in the moon drinks claret.*

## MAN OF HUNGER

(Irish *fear gorta*) An otherworldly being who wanders around, apparently in a state of malnutrition, with but little clothing, begging for alms. Those who are generous to him will be rewarded. The Man of Hunger is abroad only in times of famine.

## MANNEGISHI
In the folklore of the Cree Indians of Canada, a race of little people. They have big round heads, big eyes, no noses and skinny bodies. They are natural pranksters.

## MARA
Nightmare-producing spirit of Germanic lore.

## MÄRA-HALDDO
Spirit of the sea in Lappish lore.

## MARGOT
A name given to a fairy or fairies in Brittany.

## MASSARIOL
A diminutive being in Venetian folklore who helps on the farm and in the house.

## MAY DAY
In Welsh tradition, on this day one may visit the realm of the fairies safely. On other days human visitors are detained for one, five, seven or a hundred years.

## MAZIKIN
A term applied to winged elf*-like beings in Jewish lore. They have the powers of invisibility, precognition and shape-shifting. They eat, drink, marry, beget and die.

A tale tells how a mohel was once summoned by an otherworldly being to a dwelling inside a mountain to circumcise a baby born to a Jewish girl, who was a captive of the mazikin. She cautioned him to consume no food, else he would be unable to return to the world of men.

## MELALO
A demon in Romany lore, offspring of the Queen of the Fairies* and the King of the Devils. His appearance was that of a two-headed bird. He caused insanity. His siblings were Lilyil who

*Mermaid*

had a human head and a fish's body; Tculo, who looked like a prickly ball; Tcaridyi, who looked like a small hairy worm, etc. These were all the causes of various evils.

## MELUSINE

The supposed ancestress of the Lusignan family, she was said to be a fairy, one of three encountered by a noble hunter named Raymond. She agreed to marry him, but warned him never to look at her on Saturday. The couple had many children, but each had some deformity. One day her curious husband espied her on Saturday and saw her in the bath, discovering she had a fish or serpent tail. When he charged her with this, she left him, but would return at night to suckle her babies. Thereafter she would return at night, wailing over her castle, if a castellan were to die A variant of the tale is set in Luxembourg. Here Melusine marries Siegfroit, founder of the state. When her secret is discovered, she disappears. Because she married a human, she is now imprisoned in a rock. She appears every seven years with a key in her mouth. Whoever removes the key frees her and may wed her. She is, in durance, sewing a chemise (one stitch per seven years). If she finishes the chemise before she is freed, Luxembourg will disappear into the earth. A later romance (1478) made her mother a fairy who married the King of Scotland. They had triplets named Melusine, Melior and Plantina. She told her husband not to approach her when she was lying-in, but he, forgetfully, did so. She left him with the triplets. When the girls were fifteen they captured their father and chained him up inside a mountain called Avalon* or Brunbelois. In anger, their mother made Melusine change into a half-fish every Saturday.

## MENEHUNE

The diminutive magical beings of Hawaiian legend. They are helpful to man.

## MERMAID

The mermaid is a creature half woman and half fish. According to Scottish folklore, the fish tail is merely an outer covering, beneath which the mermaid has human legs, but this is not the general belief. Mermaids are said to possess a magic belt: if you obtain it, you can keep the owner a captive. It was sometimes thought that, if you plucked scales from a mermaid's tail, she would become a human. In England mermaids sometimes dwelt in lakes as well as in the sea. The Scots believed they could sometimes be found in rivers.

There have been various alleged sightings of mermaids, of which we can furnish some examples. In the 17th Century a man was lowered in a diving bell off the coast of the Isle o: Man. He claimed to have seen undersea buildings and streets with mermen* and mermaids gadding about.

A farmer and his family, living near Aberystwyth claimed to have seen a mermaid near their house in 1826. She was described as short-haired and very good looking. She bent down as though to take up water, after which she held her hand before her face. Her skin was very white. They saw what might have been a tail. There was a sighting in 1900 by one Alexander Gunn, a Scottish farmer. He saw a beautiful human-sized mermaid that had been stranded on the shore and was waiting for the next tide to bring her back into the sea. Her hair was reddish-yellow and her eyes greenish-blue.

A Scottish fisherman reported seeing a mermaid in 1947. She was sitting on a floating herring box, but, noting she was observed, she dived into the sea. This happened on the island of Muck.

The Mayoress of Peel, Isle of Man, and others reported seeing mermaids in 1961. The Manx Tourist Board offered a reward for a captive mermaid. There was an Irish sighting in Co Kerry in 1962.

A celebrated mermaid of a more legendary character was associated with Zennor (Cornwall). She was supposed to have fallen in love with one Matthew Trewhalla because of his voice and induced him to join her in the sea. It was later discovered that they had children. There may be some connection between this tradition and two historical churchwardens of nearby Towednack, whose carved portraits were dated 1633: their names were Matthew Trewieth and James Trwelli. Some people feel that belief in mermaids grew up because of sightings of the dugong and manatee; however, one fears that sailors who mistook these mammals for mermaids must have been visually challenged. Moreover, mermaids have been reported from areas unfrequented by either species. It is by no means impossible that there exists in the sea, as a basis for the belief, some unknown creature combining the characteristics of anthropoid and pinniped, as yet unrecognised by science.

## MERMAN
The male form of the mermaid*. There have been various reports of mermen over the centuries. Indeed, in the 19th Century there was, in the Hebrides, a family that claimed descent from a merman. A merman called the Wild Man of Orford was said to have been captured in the reign of King John (1199-1216), but escaped after six months. His diet had consisted of raw meat and fish. A Welsh farmer named Henry Reynolds who was living in 1782, claimed to have encountered a merman that looked wild and fierce, with a very sharp nose and a tail. One reported in Scotland in the 19th Century had small slant eyes, grey-green curly hair. a flat nose, large mouth and fin-like arms.

## METSHÄNHALTIA
(Finnish *metsänhaltia*, Estonian *metsheldijas*) A spirit who rules a forest. He is sometimes depicted as a greybeard. His garb is lichens. His anatomy shows great elasticity, for he can stretch as high as the topmost tree in his woodland domain.

## METSIK
Estonian forest spirit, dangerous to cattle. Sacrifices used to be made to him, to prevent his harming them.

## MEYLANDT
A name used in German romances for the country of the fairies.

*Morgan le Fay*

## MIDWIFE TO THE FAIRIES

Various folktales treat of human midwives who are used to deliver fairies of children. The 'fairies' turn out sometimes not to be fairies at all, but the human wives of fairy men. Sometimes the midwife will rub an ointment into one of her eyes which, after she has returned to humanity, enables her to see the fairy man on some occasion. He, discovering this, blinds the midwife in the eye in question.

## MOEL FAMA

Mountain in Clwyd, noted as a place where fairies dance.

## MONACIELLO

A kind of Italian sprite, of a mischievous disposition. He dresses like a monk, though he can turn himself into a cat.

## MORGAN

A sea-dwelling creature in Breton lore. Sometimes morgans are regarded as a species, male and female, but there is also a particular Morgan. She began her career under the name of Ahès or Dahut, daughter of King Gradlon of Ys. She stole the key of the floodgates which protected the city for her innamorato, the Black Prince. The gates were opened and the city was submerged, though the king escaped. His daughter became the Morgan or Marie Morgan, who was to be seen on rocks by night combing her hair. The Morgan lures sailors in boats to her, but when they reach her and she touches them, they die. Thereafter they wander through the water, their baptism removed.

## MORGAN LE FAY

Morgan is represented as the half-sister of King Arthur in Malory's *Morte d'Arthur* (1485). However, her very title Le Fay (the fairy) gives away the fact that she was considered to be a supernatural being and in some texts she is actually referred to as a goddess. She is first heard of in Geoffrey of Monmouth's *Vita Merlini* (12th Century) where Arthur, after his final battle, is taken to her to be healed. In the same century the *Roman de Troie* made her contemporaneous with the Trojan War, which indicates she was thought of as an immortal being. A clue to her origin is that in later romance she is the wife of Urien of Rheged. This Urien, according to Welsh tradition, was married to the British goddess Modron (earlier known as Matrona) and in her we have almost certainly found Morgan's origin. A mirage in the Straits of Messina is called the Fata Morgana - she was brought to Southern Italy by the Normans, who established a kingdom there.

## MOROZKO
A Russian demon of the forest. He is described as jumping from one tree to another, snapping his fingers. He is deemed responsible for frost cracks and breaks in trees.

## MOTHER OF TREES
A type of spirit in Thai folklore. There is supposed to be one in each tree. If a tree was cut down and made into a boat, it was the practice to sacrifice to the boat.

## MOURIE
The name of a spirit at Loch Maree in Scotland. There was an island in the lake containing a well at which offerings of rags and coins were left. Mourie himself was spoken of as a god and the local Presbyterian Church were none too happy to have his devotees on their doorstep.

## MUMA PADURA
It was believed that children lost in Romanian forests would be helped by this fairy.

## MUMPOKER
A frightening nursery spirit in the Isle of Wight.

## MURYAN
The muryans are found in Cornwall. They are constantly shrinking until they become ants, after which they die. This is a punishment they undergo for some unspecified transgression. They are said to be the souls of druids from long ago.

## MYDDFAI, PHYSICIANS OF

Welsh physicians, about whose origin there is a fairy legend. A young man saw a "water lady" at Llyn y Fan Fach. He tried to give her food, but she refused his baked bread. The next day he saw her again and offered her unbaked bread, but this also she refused. Then he tried slightly baked bread and this she accepted. She also accepted his proposal of marriage, but told him the marriage would come to an end if he struck her three causeless blows. These in due course were struck (all inadvertently) and the fairy returned to the lake. However, she appeared to her sons from time to time and taught them healing. This is how the Physicians of Myddfai, who are quite historical, are supposed to have had their origin. However, there is no evidence that this tale was associated with the Physicians before it was printed in 1861.

# N

## NAGA

The nagas are subterranean beings in Indian belief. A female naga is called a nagini. The lower halves of the naga race are generally serpentine, though some naginis have human legs. They have power over the element of water. Not alone do they live under the earth, but also in pools, rivers or under the sea. Some tribes assert that their ancestors were nagas. A naga can sometimes look like an ordinary snake. According to legend, the land of Cambodia was once called Kuk Thlok and consisted only of islands in a watery area. However, its king, Prah Thong, married a nagini and her father, a naga king, obligingly drank up the water.

## NARBROOI

The natives of Papua-New Guinea held this to be a spirit who dwelt in the woods. When someone fell sick, it was stated that Narbrooi had taken his soul and would need to be propitiated.

## NAT

In the folklore of Myanmar (formerly Burma) spirits are designated by this name. The spirits so called include ghosts, home-sprites*, folk heroes and even natural objects such as the sun, moon and sky. Nats who preside over rain are called *theins*. These live in the stars.

## NEGROES OF THE WATER

Legendary water dwelling beings in the folklore of Argentina, Brazil and Paraguay. Their hands and feet are webbed. They will attack craft on the water.

# NEREID

In ancient Greece, the nereids were nymphs* of the sea, the daughters of Nereus and Doris. In modern Greece, however, the term is applied to any kind of nymph*. The modern nereid can be of youthful and beauteous appearance and sometimes downright nasty. They sometimes have goats' or asses' feet. They have been known to strike people with dumbness, blindness or epilepsy or to mutilate them. They will blind and madden or else drown a man who happens to see them. They are jealous of mothers and will kill them with fever, but sometimes they will bless the child. Men sometimes marry nereids and indeed, a man can force a nereid to become his wife by stealing her clothing while she swims. In one tale a piper secured a nereid by stealing her handkerchief. She changed herself into a lion, a snake and fire to frighten him off, without success. Nereids do not make good wives for after a time they forsake husband and children. A nereid of the sea was described in 1826 as green-haired.

# NEVYN

A Welsh mermaid, very beautiful, who married a human called Ivan (?Ifan) Morgan. They had a son called Nevydd. When he discovered his mother's nature, he died of shame. This was too much for his sister Eilonwy, who threw herself into the sea in a fit of madness. However, far from drowning she became the companion of a handsome submarine knight. Meanwhile Nevydd's body was to be buried by the shore. A wave touched the coffin and out sprang Nevydd. A ship suddenly appeared and Nevydd sailed off in it.

# NIÄGRUISAR

The homesprites* of the Faeroes.

# NICKUR

A kind of water-spirit in Icelandic lore that looks like an apple-grey horse with its hooves reversed. If you get astride him he will jump into the sea. The term ninnir is also used for this kind of spirit. There may be some connection in origin with the god Odin, as Nickur was a name given to this deity.

*Nix*

## NIMBLE MEN

(Gaelic *fir clis*) Spirits of the sky in Scottish lore. They are identified with the Northern Lights. They are said to be fallen angels.

## NIS

A homesprite* found in Norway and Denmark. Nisses do work by night while the family sleeps.

## NIX

A water being in German folklore. The male has a green hat and green teeth. The female looks like a beautiful maiden. Nixes sometimes shop at markets for meat. They are well turned out, but you can see they are nixes by the small wet patch on their apparel. Nixes do not eat salt and some of them have only a single nostril. A nix requires a victim on Midsummer Day. Nixes are to be seen dancing on the water if someone is going to die.

## NJUZU

A kind of water sprite in the folklore of the Karanga of Zimbabwe. Sometimes it can look like a human-headed fish, sometimes like a destructive female who lures hapless youths to a watery doom. The njuzus have been driven from a number of pools and swamps by noise pollution. In olden times, children were sacrificed to them.

## NORK

A wood sprite found in the Tirol.

## NUCKELAVEE

An horrific figure in Scottish legend. A sea-dweller, he would come on land, blighting crops and causing pestilence to men and animals. He would also cause animals to fall off cliffs. He was repelled by fresh water, possibly because of his sea-dwelling nature, so he would never come ashore during rain. He would cause drought.

He rode upon a horse said some, others asserting that horse and rider were all one creature. He had neither skin nor hair. The horse part was endowed with flippers. He had a huge man-like head and a pig-like projecting mouth.

## NURSES TO FAIRIES

Kirk* reports that in his day there were still living women who had been taken by the fairies to nurse their children. When the fairy child is weaned, the nurse is allowed home, allowed to stay with the fairies or dies.

## NYMPH

This was a name given to sprites or nature divinities in ancient Greece. All were female and considered to be young and beautiful. There were various kinds of nymphs such as potamids (river nymphs) and orestiads (mountain nymphs). Tree nymphs were called dryads and hamadryads. It seems that at times dryads were regarded as nymphs of fruit-trees and hamadryads of oaks, but this distinction may not have been clear in people's minds, as there was a special class of fruit tree nymphs called melids. The nereids" were sea nymphs and in modern Greece the term nereid has replaced that of nymph generally.

## NYMPHIDIA

An attendant on the fairy queen Mab in the poem *Nymphidia* (1627) by Michael Drayton. She tells of how Oberon* fights with Pigwiggin over Mab until Proserpine brings an end to the proceedings. The fairies in the poem are presented as tiny beings. Puck* and Tom Thumb* make appearances.

# O

## OBERON

Oberon is most widely known for being the fairy king in *A Midsummer Night's Dream* (?1595). However, he is no invention of Shakespeare, but has a history going back several centuries. He makes his first appearance in the romance Huon de Bordeaux, where we learn he is the child of Julius Caesar and a fairy. Another fairy, uninvited to his christening, wove a spell with the result that he didn't grow taller than a three-year old child. However, she later amended this so that he grew very good-looking. In *Ysaie le Triste* we are told that he was originally a very ugly dwarf called Tronc, but the fairies gave him a kingdom and transformed his ugliness. In Drayton's *Nymphidia*, he is the husband of Queen Mab*. He appears as an underling of King Arthur in Ben Jonson's masque *Oberon the Fairy Prince*; and he is made the husband of Titania* by Shakespeare, though their marriage is not without its stormy moments.

## OGO HOLE

A cave in Shropshire, it is supposed to be the entrance to Fairyland.

## OGRE

The term ogre is somewhat loosely applied. It may signify a hairy, ugly creature, large but not quite gigantic, and definitely hostile to humans; or a giant with an appetite for human flesh; or generally any ill-visaged creature of evil. The word first appears in Perrault's *Fairy Tales* (1697). It seems to be derived ultimately from Orcus an alternative name for the Roman god Dis or Pluto*. Involved with the evolution of the idea of the ogre found in Perrault we may find the horrid Orco, found in Ariosto's *Orlando furioso* (1516). This being was eyeless, having bones sticking out where one might expect his eyes to have been. He was of gigantic proportions, but would eat only men never women, which would probably be regarded as unacceptably sexist nowadays. It seems very likely that the idea of this creature went into the concept of the ogre we find in Perrault.

## OLYROUN
A fairy king whose daughter wed the Arthurian hero Lanval.

## OMANG
Diminutive creatures in the folklore of the Batangs.

## ORANG BUNYI
These spirits of Malaysian folklore can never be seen, only heard. Hence their name of 'voice folk'.

## ORCULLO
A diminutive being in the folklore of Friuli (Italy). Orculli have shapeshifting ability.

## ORFEO
The hero of the poem *Sir Orfeo* (14th Century). The King of Winchester, Orfeo, finds that his queen, Heurodys, has been carried off by the fairies. He follows her to Fairyland. There he sees many people believed dead. Because of his musical skill, he is allowed to bring Heurodys back with him. The story is, of course, a reworking of the classical tale of Orpheus and Eurydice.

## ORIANDE
The fairy lover of Maugis d'Aygremont in the romance of that name. She is called Orianda in Italian romance.

## O'SHEA, MICHAEL
According to S. St Clair's *Mysterious Ireland* (1994), the finder in 1972 of, apparently, some fairy clothing. As the book's title would suggest, this took place in Ireland. He discovered a tiny waistcoat with a single silver button and a pair of breeches of commensurate size. Such pieces of clothing have quite often been found in Ireland.

# P

## PAMARINDO

An unpleasant diminutive being in Italian lore. He kills animals to eat by making them plunge over cliffs. His hat and shoes are of copper.

## PAN

A Greek god, half human, half goat. He is mentioned here because there seems to have been a belief at times in a whole race of pans, who occupied a place analogous to fairies in Greek beliefs. To complicate matters further, the Greeks believed in Aegipan who, some said, was Pan's father and some that he was Pan himself.

## PAPA

A Finnish spirit who brings various forms of property to humans, especially dairy products. He often appears as a cat and can actually be manufactured magically by his owner.

## PARANA DWARFS

These levitating and footless diminutive beings were reported in modern times from the Argentine city of Parana. One of the children who saw them threw a stone at one of the dwarfs and it went right through him. The dwarfs were reported to have small horns. They seem to have disappeared in a cloud of black smoke.

## PARI-BANOU

A fairy in the *Arabian Nights* who bestowed a magic tent on Prince Ahmed. This would fold up very small, but, when you spread it out, it was large enough to cover an army. She also gave him the Apple of Samarkand, a cure for any disease. Her brother Shaibar, though very small, had a thirty foot long beard

*Pan*

and two humps, one in front and one behind. He carried a heavy iron bar.

## PATUPAIAREHE

A sort of supernatural people believed in by the Maoris, somewhat difficult to distinguish from the maero*.

## PAVARO

A dog-headed elf*-like being in Italian folklore. Endowed with iron teeth and nails, he lives in bean fields, which he protects from thieves. He has very long arms, far longer than the length of his body.

## PECH(T)

The pechs are diminutive beings with long arms and red hair who live underground. They are part of the folklore of the Lowlands of Scotland. Their feet are so large they can use them as umbrellas. The construction of old buildings, such as Edinburgh Castle, is ascribed to them. The suggestion has been made that their name comes from that of the Picts, a race which inhabited Scotland in ancient and medieval times. It is interesting to note that in Northumberland the term Pict was used for a type of being intermediary between a fairy and a human.

## PEG O'NELL

A spirit said to be found in the River Ribble. She is supposed to be a ghost, but may be, in origin, the goddess of the river.

## PEG FOWLER

A spirit supposed to live in the River Tees. She has long green hair. She is always killing people. She is quite possibly the goddess of the Tees in origin.

## PEGGY WI' T'LANTHORN

This mysterious person would appear to be a kind of fairy. The Rev. S. Baring-Gould had an encounter with her in 1867 near Malham, Yorkshire. He was crossing the moors in darkness, fearful that he might plunge into a pothole, when he noted he was accompanied by a misshapen creature, later identified as a boggart*. This led him onward safely, at one time physically restraining him from from falling into a pothole. A beautiful lady with a light took his place, leading the clergyman to safety, but ever keeping a distance ahead of him. The local farmer said she was Peggy wi' t'Lanthorn.

## PHI

This term denotes classes of fairy-like beings in Thai folklore. These include beings similar to Greek tree nymphs* (*Phi nang mai*) and European homesprites* (*Chao phum phi*).

## PERI

Peris are the fairy race of Iranian lore. They also occur in other Islamic countries. Although they are regarded as good, they must have been originally evil, for their name is derived from Pahlavi *perik*, an evil spirit. They are graceful and beautiful and live in the mountains of Kâf*. Places in Peri territory include Amberabâd and Juherabâd, the cities of amber and jewels.

A tale told how Tahmuras, an ancient shah, was asked by the peris to assist them against the devas* and, mounted on the Simurgh, a giant bird, he fought against them, overcoming Arzshank their king and rescuing a female peri named Merjân, but at last being slain by a deva named Houndkonz.

## PETER PAN

A character invented by J.M. Barrie and used in his play of the same name (1904). IIe has become a personage of folklore, not alone due to the play and the book based on it, but also due to the Disney film (1953). Barrie artfully suggests that Peter is a character who has long existed in the folklore of the nursery.

Lost as a baby in Kensington Gardens*, he is taken to Neverland by the fairies, where he performs acts of derring-do against pirates and Indians. He never grows up. The influence of Pan* in his name is emphasised by his playing the panpipes and his custom, particularly evident in an unperformed screenplay written by Barrie, of riding on a goat. The play has been the object of some psychological analysis.

## PICKTREE-BRAG

A spirit who assumed the appearance of a pony and was reported from the area of Chester. If one were so unwise as to try to ride on it, he was likely to be upset into a pond, whereupon the being became unpleasantly mirthful.

## PICT
 See PECH(T)

## PILWIZ

In German lore, a supernatural being who tangles up one's hair and beard (assuming one has either or both) and inspires fear. Originally, argues Grimm, it was a good spirit, but it latterly acquired bad characteristics. The pilwiz is to be found in the mountains, his arrows feared as much as elf-shot*. The pilwizes were supposed to make cuttings in cornfields. To do this they tied sickles to their great toes and cut the corn slantwise. Legends relating to this have corrupted the name of the pilwiz into various forms (e.g. *Bilsenschnitter*, cutter of henbane). The person who wishes to deal with such vandalism must proceed with caution, if he meets the pilwiz, it must die for a year. When the sun reaches its zenith, either on Trinity Sunday or St John's Day, he must go into the field to catch his victim, making sure the pilwiz doesn't see him first, for that would be fatal. He must carry a mirror and, if the pilwiz sees him first but also sees his reflection, he will be dead for a year.

Another tradition says if you throw ears of corn cut by the pilwiz into a newly opened grave, you will stop his depredations, but the operation is fraught with peril: if you say anything or any of your perspiration enters the grave, when the ears rot you will die. If the person who owns the field where the pilwiz has reaped manages to get stubble from the reaping and hang it up in smoke, the pilwiz will waste away. The pilwiz was sometimes conceived as a human sorcerer. It dresses in linen and wears a three-cornered hat. As well as Germany, it is found further east.

*Pixy*

## PIG FAIRY

(Chinese *Chu Pa-chiai*) A character in the Chinese romance *Journey to the West*. In this tale he stands for the baser aspects of nature. He is a companion of Sun Hou-tzu a monkey, the hero of the story.

## PISACA

A kind of goblin, in Hindu mythology. Pisacas ate dead humans or uncooked flesh. They were sometimes to be seen shining in water.

## PIXY

This is the standard English form of a word often pronounced by countryfolk as pisky. The origin of the word is unknown. There is a Swedish word *pyske* meaning a small fairy which may be related. Pixies are found in Cornwall, Devon and Somerset. They are a span (hand's length) tall and wear green, with straw hats or red caps. Some said they were the souls of unbaptised infants. They take it ill if one is slovenly in housekeeping. They can turn into horses and are then called 'colt pixies'. They are often beautiful, but sometimes uncouth. They were sometimes identified with Will o' the Wisp*.

Some phenomena ascribed to pixies were of the poltergeist type. They 'pixy-ride' horses, bringing them back exhausted. They also lead people astray at night - such people are referred to as 'pixy-led'. The remedy for this is to turn your coat inside out. Pixies are ruled by a king. Those of Devon and Somerset appear to be pleasant, those of Cornwall less so. The latter were a source of annoyance and charms were used against them. Jonathan Couch, writing about 1850, said that, in his day, different kinds of beings were being referred to as pixies. Often they were spoken of as a singular noun (Pisky) and they may in origin have been a single being, a god. The Pixies' Cave on Dartmoor is said to be a pixy residence.

## PLUTO

The classical god of the underworld, he seemed to be regarded as King of the Fairies by some medieval writers. He is the fairy king

*Pooka*

in *King Orfeo* and Chaucer's *Merchant's Tale*. The unfortunate protagonist of the latter is January, an old man who marries a young bride named May. He goes blind, but Pluto restores his sight in order that he may find his wife *in flagrante* with her lover. Proserpine* the fairy queen, puts it into May's mind to tell her husband that it was all done with a view to getting Pluto to restore his sight. Pluto also rules the fairies in Drayton's *Nymphidia* (1627).

## POLEDNICE

An otherworldly being in Czech folklore, who was dangerous to women after they had given birth. She carried off one such in the form of a whirlwind and did not return her for a year.

## POLEVLK

A Russian spirit of the fields. The males have green apparel. The females are noted for their hair and dark complexions. They are clad in white beauty and can be seen at noontide.

## POLONG

In Malay folklore, a diminutive female being of the fairy kind.

## POOKA

A creature in Irish lore. It can assume any of a variety of shapes, e.g., goat, bat, and can appear as a black dog. It often takes the guise of a fierce horse which breathes blue flames and will take a rider on its back and ride around wildly until he falls off. The word pooka (also found as phooka) comes from Irish *púca*, which is thought to be a word of English origin which has supplanted some native term. Pookas are not always hostile: they can be protective to humans.

## PORTUNE

The portune, according to Gervase of Tilbury was a diminutive being in English folklore. Portunes appear to have been homesprites+, looking like old men. They were half an inch tall. Aside from working in houses, they would laugh at travellers.

## POWRIE
Another name for a dunter*.

## PROMETHEUS
One of the Titans of Greek mythology. Spenser in the *Faerie Queene* (1590-96) made him the creator of Elf, the first male of the fairy race. This Elf married a fay from the Gardens of Adonis. From them the fairy nation were descended.

## PROSERPINE
(Latin *Proserpina*, goddess of Hades) Just as Pluto* was regarded as King of the Fairies, his consort Proserpine was held to be their queen. She is found in this capacity in Chaucer and Campion.

## PUCK
A kind of elf*-like being in English lore. In Shakespeare's *A Midsummer Night's Dream* (?1595), there is only a single Puck, identical with Robin Goodfellow*. However, the name seems to have denoted a species originally. By Shakespeare Puck is classed as a tricksy sprite, going about playing pranks on mortals. The puck appears by some to have been identified as the Will o' the Wisp*. This kind of creature may have been thought of, at least by some, as an evil being.

## PUCK-HAIRY
A being, perhaps identical with Puck*, referred to in several sources since 1600. He may derive from German Pickelharing, the hero of a number of tales. In Ben Jonson's *The Sad Shepherd* (printed 1641), Puck-hairy is a witch's* familiar.

## PUKMIS
Among the Nootka Indians of North America, the pukmis were spirits of men who had nearly drowned, but had survived. A pukmis went wild in the wood after his experience of nearly dying.

## PWCA

This Welsh fairy seems to have been a homesprite* for whom food was left out. It may have been a poltergeist and identical with the bwbach*. At Cwm Pwca in Gwent, a pwca nearly led a man over a cliff, by running ahead of him with a lantern.

# Q

## QATU
The hero of a tale told in Vanuatu involving beings of fairy kind. He saw seven winged women come down to bathe. In order to do this, they divested themselves of their wings. Qatu stole the wings of one of them. She became his wife, but, on discovering her purloined wings, returned home.

## QUATERNICA
In Balkan belief, the leader of a troop of souls which appears in midwinter.

## QUEEN OF THE FAIRIES
See MAB, TITANIA, PROSERPINE.

## QUEEN OF THE FAIRIES (CONNACHT)
In Irish folklore, the King of the Fairies of Connacht, the western province, is called Finvarra*. The name of his consort is variously given as Úna (anglicised Oonagh) and Nuala.

## QUEEN OF THE FAIRIES
(Romany lore) The King of the Devils once fell in love with the Queen of the Fairies, but she rejected his suit. The devils would have destroyed the fairies, had not the queen at last acceded to his demands. Their offspring were horrible demons who brought many evils into the world. Even the King of the Devils was none too pleased with his progeny and granted her a divorce.

## QUEEN OF THE MOUNTAINS
In modern Greek folklore, a kind of tall, glistening white nereid+ who leads her followers through the hills. In Aetolia she is called Kalo (beautiful). She is perhaps in origin the goddess Artemis.

## QUEEN OF THE SHORE

In modern Greek folklore, a kind of nereid* often to be seen standing waist-high in the waters, into which she lures men by her singing to drown them.

## QUETRONAMUN

A diminutive monopod in the folklore of the Araucanian Indians of Chile and Argentina.

# R

## RAHM, PETER
The name of a 17th Century Swede whose wife, a midwife, was called upon by a little man dressed in grey, whom they recognised as a troll*. He asked her to attend his wife when she gave birth. When she went with him, she seemed to be carried by the wind. She attended the accouchement, but refused any food while there. She was wafted home and there was silver in her house next morning as a reward. Peter Rahm signed a declaration, dated 12th April 1671, asserting the truth of this tale and saying that the events in it took place in 1660.

## RAKSA
A kind of goblin* in Hindu mythology. Raksas are shape-shifters, roughly human in appearance, red-eyed and always having a deformity (e.g., two mouths, feet turned backwards). They try to kill children by adopting the guise of some kinsman of the mother and they have a taste for human flesh. They also like horsemeat. Raksas are nocturnal, the rising sun puts them to flight. They sometimes have guarding duties. Some of the sons of Yadu, who had been cursed by his father, became raksas. If a female raksa conceives, she gives birth at once, and the child has the powers of an adult. Raksa and pisaca* are interchangeable terms.

## RANZAU, COUNTESS VON
The heroine of a tale set is Schleswig (formerly in Denmark, now in Germany). She assisted a female dwarf* in giving birth. As a reward, she was given a piece of gold (to be made into fifty counters), a herring and two spindles. If these gifts were preserved, her house would enjoy good fortune. There are a number of variants of the tale.

## RAPUNZEL

The heroine of a Grimms' fairy tale, confined to a tower and accessible only by climbing her hair. Rapunzel's name means a kind of vegetable, a rampion (German *Rapunze*). It was her mother's desire for rampion when pregnant and her sending her husband to a witch's garden to procure some that was the cause of Rapunzel's troubles. With her vegetable associations, it is not impossible that Rapunzel was some sort of fertility goddess in origin.

## RAROHENGA

The country occupied by the Turehu*, a fairy race in Polynesian lore.

## REDCAP

The redcaps live in Lowland Scotland, murdering travellers who rest in peel-towers and dying their caps red with the blood of their victims. The term redcap may denote more than one kind of being.

## RED-HAIRED MAN

In Irish lore, an otherworldly being who is friendly to humans and does much to prevent their abduction to the Otherworld.

## RHOSDDU, LLYN

Lake in Anglesey. A fairy woman lived in this lake and used to bring a human woman a loaf of bread each month. In return, the human used to lend the fairy her gridiron. This arrangement came to an end when the human, despite having been warned not to do so, watched to see where the fairy went and saw her disappear into Llyn Rhosddu.

## ROBIN GOODFELLOW

A sprite in English folklore. In Shakespeare's *A Midsummer Night's Dream* (?1595) he has a broom in his hand and he may be related to the floor sweepers in the mummers' plays. He is called "he that sweeps the hearth" in the anonymous *Love Restored* (1616). He himself may have been a character in mummers'

*Robin Goodfellow*

plays. *Mad Pranks and Merry Jests of of Robin Goodfellow* (16th Century) makes him the son of Oberon*, who could change himself into animal form. When he is left a waistcoat by a maid he has been helping, he runs off. The ballad *A Monstrous Shape* (1640) says he was once a human, but the fairies tricked him into becoming one of them. Reginald Scot in his *Discoverie of Witchcraft* (1584) says he sweeps the house during the night, but is dangerous. *More Knaves Yet* (ca. 1600) claims he did not do evil.

## ROBIN HOOD

A legendary English outlaw. It has been suggested that he was a fairy sprite in origin, but this seems unlikely, due to the lack of supernatural content in the stories about him. He is more likely to be an amalgam of historical persons.

## ROBIN ROUNDCAP

A kind of sprite like Robin Goodfellow*, who flourished around Haliwell in the north of England.

## RUBENZAL

A forest demon in German lore.

## RUMPELSTILTSKIN

The well-known character of fairy tale who spins straw into gold for a damsel in distress and, in payment, demands her first child, unless she can guess his name. The name itself may have originally meant a wrinkled foreskin; but *Rumpelstilt* and *Rumpelstiltz* are found in German meaning a poltergeist (Modern German *Rumpelgeist*), which is a possible indication of the kind of creature Rumpelstiltskin was supposed to be. There are other versions of the tale in which the supernatural being is given other names, including Eisenhütel, Bonneführlein, Knirfiker, Gebhart, Tepentiren, Titteli Ture, Tom-Tit-Tot* (in England) and Trit-a-Trot (in Ireland).

## RUSALKA

(from Russian *rus*, 'river') Rusalkas are Eastern European water nymphs* (though sometimes they stray onto land) and they are generally beautiful with luxuriant green hair. They will lure men to their doom in the water and at times will tickle people, irrespective of their sex, to death. They move through the grain and dance in it. The latter activity causes an increase in its growth. They also have power over wind and rain. They appear to have exercised the function of weather divinities. The arrival of Christianity posed the question of where rusalkas fitted into the Christian cosmos. The answer seems to have been that rusalkas were girls who had somehow died outside the Church. They are held to be under the rule of the vodyanies*. Dvorak's opera *Rusalka* (1900) made the being known outside her native habitat.

# S

## SALGFRAULEIN
A spirit dressed in white in the folklore of the Tirol. She sings beneath a larch.

## SALBANELLO
A sprite in Italian lore, offspring of a salvanello* and a witch*.

## SALVANELLO
In Italian lore,offspring of a salvano* and one of the aguane*.

## SALVANO
A salvano is a male creature, human in size, but very hairy. Salvani live in the north of Italy, marry the aguane* and are protectors of the forest.

## SAMANACH
Literally, 'the Hallowe'en One'. A Scottish fairy being who would capture children at the season after which he was called.

## SAMODIVA
Samodivas are winged otherworldly beings in the folklore of Bulgaria. If you wish to capture one, you must steal her clothes.

## SANDMAN
In nursery lore, a being who brings sleep to children. Belief in the sandman was widespread in the west of Europe. In Poitou (France) this role was taken by a female, La Dormette.

## SATYR
In Greek legend, satyrs were originally much confused with silens*. Later they were clearly differentiated, having hircine

rather than equine characteristics. The satyrs originally had human feet, but these developed into hooves and satyrs were looked on as being, like Pan*, half man and half goat. There were both male and female satyrs, the latter perhaps a later development. Pliny in his *Natural History* (Ist Century AD) claimed satyrs were to be found in India and Ethiopia, but doubtless they were originally considered inhabitants of the Greek countryside.

## SCAZZAMURIEDDU

A small sprite in Italian folklore. He wears a red cap. He will sometimes indicate to humans where a treasure is hidden. He chooses human dwellings as his habitat.

## SCRAT

A supernatural creature in German lore. He was probably hairy like a satyr* and perhaps even gigantic, for Old Norse *skratti* signifies a giant. The word entered personal nomenclature in that a Thidericus Scratman was recorded in 1244. Scrats appear singly.

## SCRATTEL

This seems to be a smaller and better-tempered version of the scrat*.

## SEAL-FOLK

To all appearances these look like seals, but they can remove the sealskin to reveal a person underneath. In Ireland they are called silkies. They are seals by day, humans by night. Female silkies make good wives to humans. They have webbed fingers and toes. If you seize their cast-off skins, they must obey you.

## SEA-TROW

In Shetland and Orkney lore, a trow* which lives in the sea by the coast. He lures the wayfarer into the marsh.

## SEEHIRT

A mischievous being in Czech lore.

## SEELIE COURT

In Scotland, a term used for the good fairies, helpers and comforters of mankind.

## SHASTA, MOUNT

A mountain in California said in Native American tradition to be inhabited.by an invisible race. This race is said to be angered if anyone walks above the timberline The mountain has been the centre of other strange beliefs, for example, that there is a dwarf* city called Yaktayvia* beneath it. According to the Hopi Indians, a city built by lizard men is underneath the mountain.

## SHEBA, QUEEN OF

This Biblical personage is given a partially fairy origin in an Arab tale. Her father, the King of China, came on two snakes fighting, one black and one white He saved the white one, who turned out to be a beauteous peri*. She arranged for him to marry her sister, but stipulated he should not question her motives when she performed any action. Thus he refrained from questioning her, albeit with difficulty, when she placed their son in a fire. (He wasn't killed). When their daughter Balkis, the future Queen of Sheba was born, he made no query when his wife gave her to a she-bear; but when she destroyed the much needed food and water for his army, he could hold his peace no longer: he asked her why she had done these things. She said she had put the son in the fire to heal him of a fatal defect; that the she-bear was simply a nurse in ursine form; and that the food and water had been poisoned by a treacherous vizier. Then she disappeared.

## SHEAN

A district in Cape Breton Island (Canada), where the settlement of Inverness was founded. Here in early times large numbers of little people were said to have been seen, but they would vanish if observed. They lived on a small hill. The place name comes from Scottish Gaelic *Sithean* derived from *sith*, 'fairies'.

## SHELLYCOAT

A Scottish water spirit who was covered in shells. He could, however, doff this shelly carapace, but was then powerless. Normally he was ferocious and frightening and could fly, this causing his coat of shells to rattle.

## SHINSEEN

Beings in Chinese folklore which could appear as old men with beards or young maidens. They are benevolent and live in mountains and forests.

## SHOCK

A kind of evil spirit in English lore that could appeal in any of a number of forms. It could have a donkey's head or could appear like a calf or dog.

## SHONEY

A sea spirit to whom the inhabitants of the Isle of Lewis sacrificed a cup of ale in the hope of good fishing. This practice survived until about 1660.

## SIBILLE

(plural) Fairies who guard treasure in Italian lore.

## SIDH

(Irish *si*, Gaelic *sith*) The Sidh are the gods of ancient Gaeldom, reduced in the Christian era to the status of fairies. They were descendants of the goddess Dana, of whom little is known, and for this reason were called the Tuatha Dé Danaan, 'Danan's people'. It was said they lived in ancient burial mounds (sidhe) which gave them their name. They are also said to live in raths (early forts). They are thought of as an otherworld community, parallel with humanity. They look much like humans, but are perhaps paler. They dress richly at times, in silk or satin. Their various factions sometimes engage in battles. Belief in these fairies extends to Scotland, where Kirk* has much to say of them. He says they live under the earth, have tribes, children, nurses, marriages, deaths and burials and have light, changeable bodies, something like condensed cloud. They are said to be midway in nature between human and angel.

The following is a list of important members of the Tuatha De Danaan, who became the Sidh:-

| | |
|---|---|
| *Dana* | mother of the gods; also called Anar Anu. |
| *Dagda* | literally "the good god"; personal name *Eochaidh Ollathair;* chief of the gods. |
| *Bodb* | son of the Dagda; in later literature, King of the Tuatha Dé Danaan |
| *Boinn* | goddess of the River Boyne. |
| *Diancecht* | the physician. |
| *Goibniu* | the smith. |
| *Manannan* | god of the sea. |
| *Ogma* | inventor of the Ogham script. |
| *Brigit* | the poetess. |
| *Nuada* | King of the Tuatha Dé Danaan. |
| *Crindbel* | the satirist. |
| *Aengus* | son of the Dagda. |
| *Lugh* | expert in many arts; slayer of the giant* Balor. |
| *Morrigan* | war goddess; wife of the Dagda; perhaps originally identical with Dana. |

## SIGVARD FOSTRE

The protagonist of an Icelandic tale who made an elf*-woman pregnant. He said if she brought the baby to church, he would have it baptised. She did so, leaving the child there, but Sigvard did not acknowledge paternity and even told the pastor not to baptise it. The elf-woman, furious, cursed him and his descendants until the ninth generation.

## SILEN

The silens, creatures of Greek myth, were old and had the ears of horses. Sometimes they may have been thought to have the tails and legs of horses as well. At first there was confusion between silens and satyrs* and even latterly the siren Marsyas had caprine rather than equine characteristics.

## SILVAN

The Romans had a nature god called Silvanus, who was sometimes identified with Pan* and Faunus. He had under his protection live trees and the borders of fields and he would sometimes carry a cypress about with him. He was regarded as aged. The silvans were a pluralised form of Silvanus and, as nature spirits, they occupied the place of fairies in Roman belief. They were half man, half goat like the fauns*, but were larger in stature.

## SINISTRARI, LOUIS MARIE

(1622-1701) A Franciscan whose *Daemonalitas* argues that there are spiritual animals of an intermediate nature between men and angels, capable of good and evil. These beings approximate somewhat to the concept of fairies. He says their bodies are each formed largely of one of the four elements. Sinistrari uses the term demons to denote them, but he appears to employ this term to mean simply spirits.

## SIREN

Sirens are rather grotesque creatures in Greek mythology. There were two to four of them, human from the thigh up and bird from the thigh down. They had the most beautiful singing voices, by which they would lure sailors ashore and then kill them. The Argonauts sailed past them due to the music of Orpheus, which was sweeter than their notes. Odysseus heard their song by having himself tied to the mast of his ship as he sailed by them, so he would not jump overboard, his crew having plugged their ears. In a number of languages words derived from *siren* are used to signify a mermaid.

## SKOGSRA

Skogsras are female sprites, small in stature, in Swedish folklore. Generally benevolent, a skogsra would be unfriendly to a hunter, unless offered part of his catch. Skogsras have claws in place of nails.

## SKREE

A monster with red eyes and wings, black in colour and leathery in appearance. The night before the Battle of Culloden (1746) it was seen shrieking over the opposing armies. Lord George Murray was one of those who saw it.

## SKY SPIRITS

Beings in Rarotongan folklore who taught the hero Ngaru how to play ball games.

## SORCHA

Irish, 'bright'. The name of an otherworldly country in Irish lore containing a City of Gold.

## SPIDER-WOMAN

A creature in Japanese lore which could assume various forms, but who would entrap her victims in a sticky net. She was killed by a hero called Raiko.

## SPRIGGAN

A diminutive being in Cornish folklore. Spriggans are mischievous by nature and kill children. They are the ghosts of giants*. They can change their size if they wish. Spriggans are said to guard a giants' treasure at Trencrom Hill, Cornwall.

## STAR SPIRITS

Spirits adhering to artificial stars, used by Thais to protect their crops from the depredations of animals.

## STOCK

In Scotland and Ireland, fairies carrying off women or children would sometimes leave a carving of the abducted one, usually made out of wood, in lieu. One Irish story tells how a man was kidnapped by the fairies and a false man sent home in his place.

## STRENTU

A kind of giant* believed in by the Huron Indians. Strentu had protective scales on their bodies and had cannibalistic tendencies.

## SULEVIA

A kind of female spirit in the belief of the ancient Gauls.

## SWAN MAIDENS

Women who turn into or are turned into swans. Such women feature in a number of tales. The Valkyries of Odin in Norse mythology had swan suits, which they could don and doff as they wished. A German tale tells of a swan maiden who was captured by a nobleman who managed to do this by stealing her necklace. She gave birth to seven children at one time and all could turn into swans.

In the Irish story of the Children of Lir, the children (one of whom was male) were turned into swans by a wicked stepmother. Evil swan maidens, demons in fact, were believed in amongst the Tartars. Though there were forty of them, they would converge into a single huge swan.

## SYLPH

According to Paracelsus, an elemental spirit of the air

## SYLVESTER

According to Paracelsus, a spirit of the woods.

# T

## TALON-HALTIJA

A spirit, sometimes ancestral, who guards the house in Finnish lore.

## TAM LIN

A hero of balladry, who was captured by the Queen of the Fairies. While he did not find the fairy realm a bad place to live in, every seven years the fairies gave one of their number as a tribute to the Devil and he feared he would be next. Janet, the daughter of a mortal king, became enamoured of and pregnant by him. Tam told her how she could rescue him from the fairies: as they rode past at midnight on Hallowe'en, she should pull him from his horse. This she did and so Tam was won back from the fairies.

## TAWA-O-HOI

An evil maero* in Maori tradition. He was regarded as a chieftain of a pre-Maori race in New Zealand. He had a tendency to eat Maoris so he was buried under Mount Tarawera by a famous priest, Ngatoro-i-rangi. He then became the spirit of Mount Tarawera.

## TAMARA

A nymph*in Cornish folklore, the object of the affections of the two sons of Dartmoor giants*, who urged her to choose between them. Her father, a subterranean being, cursed her when she refused to leave them and she became the River Tamar, in olden times the boundary between Cornwall and England, of which Cornwall was not then considered part.

## TAROGOLO

A kind of sexual but destructive spirit in the folklore of the Lakalai of New Britain for, not alone does he seduce humans, but he destroys their sexual parts.

## TARW, LLYN

A lake in Powys which was supposedly a haunt of the little people. Strange, sweet singing was heard there as recently as 1936.

## TATERMAN

A sprite in Germanic folklore, J. Grimm opines that the original form of the word may have been *katerman* (cat man) and that he was a helpful sprite of the Puss-in-Boots variety. However, this is less likely if the Austrian German *tatterman* (bugbear, scarecrow) and Scots *tatty-bogle* (scarecrow) are related to it. It is also possible the term originally meant 'doll, puppet' and is connected with Magyar *tatos* (juggler).

## TEIND

In Scottish belief, a tribute of a person paid by the fairies every seven years to the Devil. Both Thomas the Rhymer and Tam Lin were aware of the possibility that they might be the victim. In both cases the largeness of the men is alluded to, which leads L. Spence to the consideration that there might be a recollection of cannibalism here. The teind is also called a kain (Gaelic *cain*).

## TERDELASCHOYE

A fairy in the *Parsifal* of Wolfram von Eschenbach (fl. 1200). She is really Morgan Le Fay*, but, owing to poor knowledge of French , Morgan's country, *Terre de la Joie*, was thought to be the fairy's name and Terdelaschoye is a German form of this.

## THOMAS THE RHYMER

An historical person who flourished in Scotland somewhere between the last years of the 12th and 13th Centuries His surname was 'de Erceldoun'. He was supposed to have predicted the death of King Alexander III in 1286; however, the actual prediction may have been about the weather. He had a reputation as a prognosticator, who was supposed to have acquired his abilities from his dealings with the fairies. The legendary history of Thomas is to be found in a romance of the 15th Century and a ballad of the 18th Century.

When Thomas was lying on Huntlie Bank, the tale runs, he saw the Queen of the Fairies. He made love to her and she changed into a hag. She could now force him to go with her. She brought him under Eildon and brought him into a garden, where fruit abounded, but all of it was cursed. She showed him ways to Heaven, Paradise, Purgatory and Hell and the castle on a hill where the King and Queen of the Fairies lived. Her beauty returned, they went to Fairyland. Thomas was told not to speak. He stayed there three Years, but thought it was only three days. Then the Queen returned him to humanity, for fear he would be selected for the teind*. She gave him the gift of a tongue that could not lie so he became a prophet.

A legend told about Thomas is that, like King Arthur and Frederick Barbarossa (to mention but two), he is still alive under a hill and will, at some future date, emerge to fight a great battle, becoming king. It is said that one moonlit night a horse-coper named Canobie Dick was stopped by an aged man who bought two horses from him and over a period bought more. The old man eventually took Dick into an Eildon hill called Lucken Hare. Inside were knights in black armour with black horses. The old man identified himself as Thomas the Rhymer. There were a sword and a horn on a nearby table. Thomas said whoever drew the sword and winded the horn would be King of Britain, provided he did these things in the right order. Unfortunately perhaps fortunately - Dick made the wrong choice, blew the horn first and was whisked out of the cave by a whirlwind. He died after gasping out his story to some shepherds. The suggestion has been made that Thomas from time to time went to stay in monasteries and his periodic absences gave rise to the original notion that he went to Fairyland.

## THRUMMY-CAP

A kind of sprite, resembling an old man, in the folklore of Northumberland. He was often found in cellars.

## TIDDY-MUN

In the Fens , marshy areas in Eastern England, the Tiddy-Mun was a kind of spirit. He was described as an old man with white hair and a matted beard of the same colour. He was invoked to calm the waters of the Fens. He objected so much when the Fens were drained that he had to be propitiated. Sometimes he is spoken of in the plural (Tiddy men)

## TIME

In the realm of the fairies, time seems to be different from that of our world. Beings who sojourned with the fairies found, on their return, that a much longer period of time had passed than they had thought. Illustrations of this will be found in the articles on Herla* and Thomas the Rhymer*.

To show how far flung this idea is, a Chinese book by Tu Kuang-t'ing (850-933) describes how a man entered one of the "cave heavens" and stayed there for what did not seem a long time, but when he returned to the human world, nine generations had passed.

## TÍR NA nÓG

(Irish, 'Land of the Young') A land of perpetual youth, an otherworldly realm, in Irish legend, known as *Eilean na hOige* in Scotland. It seems to have been a Celtic paradise. Thither went Ossian (Oisin), the poet of the Fianna, brought by an otherworldly lady named Niamh. When he returned to Ireland he was warned not to dismount from his horse, but did so accidentally and found he was now an old man. In one version, he crumbled into dust. He had not aged in Tír Na nÓg, but the aging process caught up with him on his return to his native soil.

## TITANIA

The fairy queen in Shakespeare's *Midsummer Night's Dream* (?1595). Her marriage to Oberon* had its stormy moments. She is of classical origin in that her name was originally an epithet applied by Ovid to the goddesses Diana, Circe and Latona.

## TOKOLOSHE

(Xhosa *tikoloshe*, Afrikaans *tokkelossie*) A kind of goblin* in South African lore, which has been described as half-man, half-beast and the abominable snowman of the veld. The tokoloshe is about the size of a baboon and is credited with the power of invisibility. Because of this, it has sometimes been said tokoloshes aid burglars.

## TOMALIN

A fairy knight in Drayton's *Nymphidia* (1627), related to Oberon*.

## TOM-NA-HURICH HILL

A hill on the outskirts of Inverness, in which fairies are supposed to dwell. Once the Queen who ruled them tried to make a mortal her husband, but he refused, as he loved his wife and child. The Queen let him go - he had been careful not to eat any fairy food - but on his return home he found his family missing. They had been taken into the hill. A kindly fairy told him to sing a certain song at the hill and, when he did so, his wife and child would be pushed out of the hill door. When fiddlers were taken into this hill to play for the fairies and thought they had played for but a single night, on their emerging they found they had been gone for a hundred years and had aged accordingly. A look in the mirror caused them considerable shock. The local minister blessed them and they crumbled into dust.

## TOM THUMB

He seems originally to have been a being of the fairy kind in folklore. Scot in his *Discoverie of Witchcraft* (1584) so classifies him. The standard story of Tom makes him merely an abnormally small being. This appeared in a booklet in 1621.

This tells us that he was conceived with the help of Merlin and the Queen of the Fairies was the midwife at his birth.

## TOM-TIT-TOT

The English equivalent of Rumpelstiltskin*.

## TOMTE

A dwarfish homesprite*, found in Sweden. His name is a shortened form of *tomtgubbe* (old man of the house).

## TOOTH FAIRY

It is widely believed in nursery lore that, when a child loses a first tooth, if this is left under his pillow it will be collected by the tooth fairy who will leave money in its place. In the author's experience, the tooth fairy these days is managing to keep abreast of inflation.

## TRASGU

A homesprite* in the folklore of North-West Spain. The trasgu is attached to the family rather than to the house it inhabits and will follow it when it moves. It is of diminutive stature and wears red.

## TRIUNNIS NAGELWCH

In a Welsh story related by Walter Map (fl. 1200) we are told that this worthy was the son of a human father and a fairy mother. As is frequently the case in tales of such marriages, the father broke some taboo on which the union's continuance depended. The fairy fled with their children, but the father managed to save one, Triunnis. When an adult, Triunnis, given a military command, was defeated, but saved by his mother, afterwards dwelling in the lake from which she had magically come.

## TROLL

The derivation of the word is uncertain. It may be related to Swedish *troll* (bewitch) and Old Norse *trolldómr* (witchcraft), giving it magical connections. These are reinforced by the fact that in Lappish magic an article called a trolldrum was used. In early Scandinavia trolls were giants*, who went about by night for, if the sun shone on them, they would turn to stone.

In modern folklore they are diminutive beings who live in hills and mounds, sometimes called Bjergfolk. They are helpful and friendly, but sometimes steal children, women or possessions. They are rich, dwelling in houses of gold or crystal. They hate noise. They have powers of invisibility, shapeshifting and prognostication.

## TROW

A trow is a grey-clad diminutive being in the folklore of Shetland and Orkney. The term is a corruption of the Scandinavian *troll**. Should you espy a trow, it will walk backwards while you look at it. A young trow is called a trowling. Trows can become invisible. They live in knowes (small hills). Inside these knowes are much gold and silver. To dance, a pastime in which they love to indulge, they crouch and hop about. One of their great feasts is Midsummer Eve. They are let out of the underworld about Yuletide, but have to return there on Up-helly-aa.

## TUATHA DÉ DANAAN

See SIDH.

## TUREHU

Fairies, fair of hair, in Polynesian belief. One of them was said to have married a prince called Mataora and, though their marriage was happy, he once abused her and she returned to her homeland. There are parallels here with European tales of fairy marriages, but, unlike the usual heroes of them, Mataora at length won his bride back. He brought back from the country of the turehu knowledge of tattooing and weaving.

## TWEEDIE

This individual in Scottish legend was the son of the water spirit of the River Tweed. His mother was the Baroness of Drumelzier. She was violated by the spirit while her husband was away on the Crusades. When the husband returned, he adopted the boy

*Trow*

who became the next baron. In Scotland, persons with the surname Tweedie claimed descent from the son of the Tweed.

## TYLWYTH TEG

(Welsh, 'fair family') A race of Welsh fairies who visit the earth, yet are not of it. Some say they can fly. Some hold they are small, some that they are larger. They hunt on grey horses, will sometimes do domestic tasks, abduct children and purloin cheese and butter. One account says they are dwarfs*, mainly female, who wear white and are ruled by King Gwydion and Queen Gwenhidw. This Gwydion son of Don was a god of the ancient British. The Tylwyth Teg are said in some places to live in a country ruled by a mysterious character called Rhys Dwfn. This country could only be seen if one stood on a square yard of land with certain herbs in it. These same herbs were used by the Tylwyth Teg to render themselves invisible. The Tylwyth Teg were known as *Plant Rhys Dwfn* (Children of Rhys Dwfn) and used to buy things from humans, until the latter started charging too much.

# U

## UCAKIJANA

A kind of dwarf* in Zulu and Xhosa folklore. His mother is human. He is noted as a prankish being and has the power to disappear. He is also called Hlakanyana. Among the Tsonga he is called Mpfundlwa.

## UIIRKSAK

A kind of spiritual husband believed in by the Eskimo. Sometimes their unions with human women are fruitful. There seems to be nothing amiss with the offspring. The female equivalent is the nuliarksak. She will become the spirit wife of a man, but their children are not seen. Presumably they are raised in the otherworld.

## ULK

Term applied to elf*-like beings in the Baltic region. The female is called an ulkwife.

## UNDINE

A term used to mean a water spirit or nymph*, derived from Latin *unda*, a wave. It was used as the personal name of a water-nymph in the novel *Undine* (1807) by De La Motte Fouqué. It tells how Undine, a changeling*, was married to the knight Huldebrand, thereby gaining a soul; but, when he told her off, she was reclaimed by her fellow spirits. When Huldebrand was to marry another, Undine entered his chamber from a well, kissed him and he died. When they buried him a silver stream, Undine in liquid form, appeared about his grave.

## UNSEELIE COURT

A Scottish name for the wicked fairies.

## URCHIN

The word actually means a hedgehog, but it was formerly used to mean a being of the fairy kind. Lewis Spence thinks it may be traced back to the Anglo-Saxon orcneas, creatures mentioned in the poem *Beowulf* (?8th Century).

## URGAN

In Sir Waiter Scott's *Lady of the Lake* (1810), this is the name bestowed on Ethart, stolen as a child by the King of the fairies, but freed from bondage by his sister Alice.

## URGANDA

A celebrated good fairy in the romance of *Amadis de Gaul* (15th Century), in which she supports Amadis, the hero.

## URISK

(Gaelic *uruisg*) A variously described kind of being in Scottish legend. Urisks are male and female and are seen by people with second sight. Some say they are large and live in the mountains and other unfrequented areas. They are sometimes said to be shaggy and satyr*-like, resembling Pan in that they are part man, part goat. They fought against the Highlanders on occasion. Another description says the urisk has yellow hair, a long staff used for walking and a blue bonnet. It is not unknown for an urisk to be a homesprite.

## URSITORY

Spiritual beings in Gypsy lore. Three days after a child is born, three ursitory appear and map out his destiny.

# V

## VANADEVATA
A spirit which inhabits a tree in Indian lore.

## VAZILA
In Slavic belief, the vazila is a small hairy being with horse's ears and hooves. Domiciled as a rule in the stable, the vazila cares for horses on a farm.

## VED
A large, hairy man-like being in Croatian folklore. The ved is very tall - it is said larger than a house - and wears ragged clothes. Veds in the old days could be helpful, often attaching themselves to a particular human, but some were of a wild and intractable nature and had been known to capture humans and reduce them to serfdom, but they would eventually release them. The bones of dead veds were sometimes discovered. Their contact with humans grew less and less from about the beginning of the 20th Century.

## VEDENHALTIA
A water spirit in Finnish lore.

## VESNA
In Slovene belief, women of the fairy kind called vesnas inhabit mountain palaces and direct the fate of men. They also make decisions concerning the crops.

## VETTE
In Danish lore, a female spirit of the woods.

## VILA

The plural of vila is *vile* and these are fairy-like beings amongst the Serbs, Croats and Slovenes. They live in the mountains and are long-haired and beautiful, wearing white. Some say their mothers are fairies, made pregnant by the due; others, that they come from plants. Their voices sound like those of woodpeckers. They collect storms in the sky. They sometimes have the legs of an animal and they can change into animal shapes. They take part in a kind of dance called *kolo*; intrude upon it at your peril.

## VITRA

A female troll* in a Swedish story. The tale tells that a human midwife was summoned to assist her in giving birth. This she did; but she refused to accept any food in the troll's dwelling. This was a grand house and Vitra herself a beautiful lady. She urged the midwife to take payment, but the latter refused. However, she was later rewarded with silver spoons.

## VITTORE

A homesprite* in Albanian folklore, regarded as looking like a small snake.

## VIVIAN

In Arthurian lore, she is noted as the lady with whom Merlin fell in love. She was also called Nimue, the two names originally perhaps having been the same, altered by scribes in error. In Brittany she seems to have been revered as a fairy until modern times. A female wood-gatherer there told in 1910 how Vivian had saved her husband from gamekeepers by sending a fog which encompassed him and whispering to him that the spirit of Vivian would protect him until he had left the forest.

## VODYANY

This is the name of an Eastern European water being. The vodyany's appearance is generally off-putting as he is fat, ancient and ugly. He is generally disagreeable and will cause storms. If you are so unfortunate as to drown in the vicinity of a vodyany, he will eat your body and store your soul in a jar. A vodyany may try to pass himself off as human, but, if the observer watches him closely, he will see that the tip of his shirt is wet and that he has left a puddle in his chair.

## VOLLMAR
See GOLDEMAR

## VOUGH
An anglicised form of fuath*.

# W

## WACHHOLDER, FRAU

In German folklore, the spirit of the juniper. She could be invoked by a ritual to make a thief surrender what he had stolen.

## WAG AT THE WA'

A supernatural creature which suffered the dreadful affliction of perpetual toothache. To ease his woe, he held his nightcap over the afflicted part of his face. He was to be found in kitchens and looked like a little old man with a long tail. He flourished around the English/Scottish border.

## WACHILT

A sea-dwelling being who was an ancestress of Widia, the son of Wayland*. She saved Widia from danger by bringing him to the sea-bed, where she lived.

## WALDGEISTER

A kind of spirit supposed to live in the forests of Germany. Some are good and some evil. They are versed in the secrets of medicinal plants.

## WATERMAIDS

In the *Nibelungenlied* (13th Century), such beings (German *Merewiper*) were encountered in the Danube by the Burgundians. One of them named Madeburch had powers of prophecy, perhaps a general attribute of this kind of being.

## WANAGEMESWAK

Water-dwelling little people in the folklore of the Penobscot Indians. They are so thin that you cannot see one facing you, only when it turns sideways.

## WANG CHIH

A Chinese noted in Taoist lore. One day he came upon some elderly men playing chess. They gave him a piece of food resembling a date stone to eat. Eventually, they told him to leave. On returning to civilization, he found he had been absent for centuries. The chess-players were otherworldly beings and the tale is one of those which would indicate that otherworldly time* goes at a different pace from ours.

## WAYLAND

A goldsmith and blacksmith in Germanic mythology. Wayland is described as an elf*. It was said that Wayland's father, Wade, a giant*, entrusted him to the dwarfs*. The understanding was that they could kill him if Wade did not return in a certain time. Unfortunately Wade himself was killed, so Wayland had to escape in a marvellous boat. He was captured by King Nidudr who made him lame. However, he escaped after killing Nidudr's sons. He fashioned cups from their skulls and raped the king's daughter. Then he flew away through the air by magic. The king's daughter gave birth to a son called Widia. Wayland was the smith of the Germanic gods. A megalithic tomb in Oxfordshire is called Wayland's Smithy.

## WELLS

Wells are sometimes thought to be the dwellings of fairies or similar beings. A Welsh story has a young man washing his face in one, disappearing and thereafter seen dancing with the fairies. He was rescued by friends, but disappeared for a while thereafter and returned with a wife who was suspected of being a fairy, as she was very good-looking. The well spirit at Tarbat (Gigha, Hebrides) was invoked to provide a fair wind. A local person had to remove the covering of stones of the well and clean it with a bowl or clam shell. Then the water was thrown in the direction from which the wind was desired. Two old women were in charge of the ceremonial. The spirit of the well at Tobar-nim-buadh (St Kilda) was the recipient of a cultus that lasted as late as the mid-18th Century. To a well at Inverness were brought children thought to be changelings". The Pin Well near Woolen contained fairies and girls would drop crooked pins into it.

# WENDI
Another name for the ihk'al*, used in Belize.

# WIGHT
Although this word simply means a creature, it is often used to mean a supernatural creature. Thus Chaucer couples elves* with wights in *The Miller's Tale*. In the year 830, according to one Cornelius à Kempen, there were female wights all over the place. They tended to abduct children. In the southern reaches of Germany, there was a class of dwarfish beings referred to as wights (German *Wichtlein*).

# WILD EDRIC
An historical personage who lived in the reign of the Conqueror, whom he opposed with arms. Legend made him the husband of a fairy, saying that he had come on a house where tall and beautiful women were dancing. He abducted one and she agreed to marry him, but said she was never to upbraid him about her place of origin or her sisters. After many years of marriage, he chided her for tarrying with her sisters when she came home late one evening and she left him.

Edric was supposed not to have died, but to be seen riding with his wife and train before the outbreak of war. An eyewitness claimed to have seen this phenomenon in 1853/4 before the Crimean War. His wife, accompanying him, is called Lady Godda - compare Frau Gauden, a leader of the German Wild Hunt*.

# WILD HUNT
A collection of wild supernatural raiders in folklore. It is given various leaders. In Germany it was sometimes led by the god Woden. Elsewhere in the same country its leader was called Hackelbrand. He is supposed to have been Hans von Hacklenberg, a hunter, who died in 1521 (or 1581), mortally wounded by a boar's tusk. On his death bed he said he did not want Heaven but hunting. The minister said he must then hunt until Doomsday. Under the name of Hackelberg he became a hunter, but J. Grimm feels that Hacklenberg is derived from an epithet applied to Woden.

In the north-east of Germany, the wild huntsman was called Wed. To avoid his (generally unpleasant) attentions, the night-time wayfarer was urged to keep to the middle of the road where he would be untroubled. Another German leader of the hunt was Frau Goden. She had twenty-four daughters. Because she and her daughters loved hunting more than the thought of Heaven, she became the wild huntress, four of her daughters becoming horses pulling her carriage, the rest hounds.

Cross-roads are dangerous to Frau Goden. If she comes into one, her carriage breaks. In fact, she appears to have come into existence because of a mistake: Frau Goden represents an earlier Frau Woden derived from a masculine *fro Woden*.

Theodoric the Goth (died 451) under his legendary name of Dietrich of Bern is also said to captain the Hunt. Other German leaders of it are Hans Jagenteufel, Mansberg and Martin the Hunter. It is also found in France, led by Charlemagne with Roland carrying his standard or by Hellekin from whom Harlequin* is said to have developed; in Britain where it is led by King Arthur; and in Spain where it is called the Old Army and identified with the dead.

## WILD MAIDENS
(German *Wilden Fraulein*) Golden-haired, blue-eyed white-garbed and above all extremely beautiful sprites of South Germany and Western Austria. Of these the Seligen Fraulein are often pursued by wild men* who seek to destroy them. They love bells. Another variety, the Dialen, have the feet of goats.

## WILD MEN
Wild men were hairy creatures of the wodewose* variety, in whom there was widespread belief in the Middle Ages. J. Grimm cites the writer Machar who says that, in his time, there were wild men in the valley of the Gastein in living memory. The term is also applied to weather giants* in the folklore of the Tirol.

# WILD WOMEN

(German *Wilde Frauen*) These beings were said to live beneath the Wunderberg, near Salzburg (Austria). The mountain was said to be hollow and to contain a wondrous country, housing, besides the Wild Women themselves, giants*, little people and the Emperor Charles V, who, far from dying as is generally thought by historians, sits there with knights and nobles in attendance. Legend had it that, about the year 1753, the Wild Women were wont to emerge and feed children herding animals. Once they were said to have taken away a boy who was a cowherd. The boy was espied about a year thereafter, clad in green.

# WILL O' THE WISP

The common name for the ignis fatuus, a light glimpsed over marshes. In folklore it is thought to be an actual being of some sort.

# WILLIAMS, EDWARD

(1750-1813) Welsh clergyman who claimed to have encountered diminutive, elfin beings as a child. He was with four other children, when he saw these beings dancing in a field at noon. They wore red and had reddish kerchiefs about their heads. They seemed smaller than the children. One of them started to give chase. The children bolted, leaving the field by way of a stile. Williams had a good look at his pursuer, whom he described as "swarthy and grim".

# WITCHES

Sometimes in days gone by witches or those accused of witchcraft, claimed to have commerce with the fairies rather than the Devil. Perhaps they thought they would be punished less severely for this. E. Pócs argues that in the south-east of Europe, belief has transferred to witches the evil characteristics of the fairies.

## WODEL

A term designating an evil kind of spirit in Chermessian folklore. Wodels could be found in the water, in fire and in the air.

## WODEWOSE

A shaggy kind of wild man* in Anglo-Saxon lore. Wodewoses appeared to be subhuman and incapable of speech. A wodewose's diet included children he happened to catch and they were known to carry off women. Wodewoses were used in heraldry.

## WOKULO

Diminutive 3' high beings in the folklore of the Bammana of Mali. They are largely invisible and have big hairy hands. They are subject to a devil named Dume.

## WOMAN OF THE MIST

This Somerset spirit is sometimes seen as an old woman. She is supposedly seen in autumn and winter on a road going over a hill at Loxey Thorne. There were appearances of her reported in 1920 and in the 1950s. She fades into mist.

## WOODFOLK

In Southern German lore, diminutive beings who, not surprisingly inhabit the woods. Moss forms their clothing. They are grey and of oldish appearance, but greater in size than elves*. The females beg or steal food from woodcutters. If a man twists a young tree, detaching the bark, one of the females dies. Sometimes a wood woman pushes a wheel-barrow in front of her. Fix it for her and she will pay in chips which later turn to gold.

## WOODLAND MAIDENS

(Croatian *sumske dekle*) These are hair-covered beings in the folklore of Croatia. Though their shrieks are audible in the woods, they have never been heard to talk. They are grateful if humans leave out food for them and will show their gratitude by work (such as sweeping the house).

*Woodwose*

*Wood-Wife*

## WOOD-WIFE

(German *Holz-frau*) Wood-wives are beings in German legend who in days gone by at least would often accept food from people. They were sometimes known to approach someone with a small wheel-barrow, asking him to repair it. They are chased by the Wild Huntsman and will seek safety by hiding in a tree with a cross on it. Germans believed that on Ash Wednesday the Devil would chase wood-wives. Sometimes at least a wood-wife was of shaggy appearance, with moss all over her.

## WRYNECK

A spirit in the north of England, believed to be very evil.

## WULVER

A quite benevolent creature in the lore of Shetland. He has the body of a man and the head of a wolf. He inhabits a cave and is much given to fishing. He will sometimes leave fish on a window-sill for a poor person.

## WUT-IA

A water spirit in Chermessian folklore. The wut-ia has, at least sometimes, a beautiful daughter who dwells in the sea.

# X Y Z

## XANA
A female nature spirit found in Asturias (Spain). Xanas occupy caves and mountains. They are small of stature and long-haired. In some cases, they are women who have been placed under a spell.

## YAKSA
A kind of goblin* in Hindu lore, different from, but very similar to, a raksa*.

## YAKTAYVIA
In Californian folklore, a city beneath Mount Shasta*, populated by dwarfs*, whose magic bells are said to be audible at times.

## YARTHKIN
An alternative name for the Tiddy-Mun*.

## YELLOW DWARF
A malignant being in one of Countess d'Aulnoy's *Fairy Tales* (1682). He abducted a princess on his Spanish cat and managed to kill her betrothed intentionally and her lover by accident. His name was derived from his colour and the fact that he lived in an orange tree.

## YOSEI
Term for fairies used in Japan.

## YVONNE
Heroine of a Breton fairy tale. Her father had, in addition to her, six sons, but she and the youngest son, Yvon, were badly treated. One day, she disappeared. The five elder brothers sought her,

but in vain. Yvon, however, found her living with a husband in a palace. When he at last returned home, he found that generations had passed since his departure. He had been in a fairy realm. This is another story illustrating how time in the land of Faerie differs from our time.

## ZINA

A term for a fairy used, with differing pronunciations, by the Romanians and Albanians. The Albanians also use the terms *zana, zera*. These are all derived from the name of Diana, the Roman goddess of the chase. A notable Zina is Zina Magdalina, who sits in a tree, perhaps a mythological world tree.

## ZIP

A zip is a diminutive being in the folklore of Mexico. Zips are apparently warriors, for they wear helmets and carry spears. They look after deer.

## ZLATA BABA

Leader of troops of souls appearing about Midwinter in Balkan countries.

## ZMEJ

A kind of ancestral spirit in Slavic legend. He appears in animal form and fathers on a human mother a human zmej, a kind of wizard.

## ZORPHEE

A fairy godmother* in the romance of *Amadis of Gaul* . Her goddaughter Niquee formed an incestuous connection, so Zorphee had to place her under a spell to break this off.

# BIBLIOGRAPHY

Arrowsmith, N. *A Field Guide to the Little People* London, 1977.
Baring-Gould, S. *Curious Myths of the Middle Ages* Oxford, 1894.
Bartrum, P.C. *A Welsh Classical Dictionary* n.p., 1993.
Benwell/Waugh *Sea Enchantress* London, 1961.
Black, J. *History's Mysteries* Edinburgh, 1993.
Bord, J. and C. *The Enchanted Land* London, 1995.
Brandon, J. *Weird America* New York, 1978.
Briggs, K.M. *The Anatomy of Puck* London, 1959.
Briggs, K.M.*The Fairies in Tradition and Literature* London, 1967.
Brooks, J.A. *Ghosts and Legends of Wales* Norwich, 1987.
Bryant, P. *The Aquarian Guide to Native American Mythology* London, 1991.
Clark, J. *Unexplained!* Detroit, 1993.
Cockerton, F. *The Pixy Book* Penryn, 1996.
Coghlan, R. *Encyclopaedia of Arthurian Legends* Shaftesbury, 1991.
Coghlan, R. *Pocket Dictionary of Irish Myth and Legend* Belfast, 1985
Coleman, L. *Curious Encounters* Boston, 1985.
Colombo, J.R. *Mysterious Canada* Toronto, 1988.
Edwards, G. *Hobgoblin and Sweet Puck* London, 1974.
Floyd, E.R. *More Great Southern Mysteries* Little Rock, 1990.
Grimm, J. *Teutonic Mythology* New York, 1966.
Hartland, E.S. *The Science of Fairy Tales* London, 1891.
Hopkins, E.W. *Epic Mythology* Strasbourg, 1915.
Hunt, R. *Popular Romances of the West of England* London, 1865.
Keightley, T. *Fairy Mythology* London, 1850.
Kirk, Robert *The Secret Common-wealth* Cambridge, 1976.
Knappert, J. *Indian Mythology* London, 1991.
Knappert, J. *Pacific Mythology* London, 1992.
Koppana, K.M. *TheFinnish Gods* Helsinki, n.d.
Lawson, N. *Modern Greek Folklore and Ancient Greek Religion* Cambridge, 1910.
Leach, M. *Funk and Wagnall's Standard Dictionary of Folklore Mythology and Legend* London, 1975.
Lum, P. *Fabulous Beasts* London, n.d.
MacManus, D.A. *The Middle Kingdom* London, 1959.
Marinacci, M. *Mysterious California* Los Angeles, 1988.
Mayer, D. *Harlequin in his Element* Cambridge, Mass., 1969.

Opie, I. and P. *The Classic Fairy Tales* London. 1951.

Pócs, E. *Fairies and Witches at the Boundary of South-Eastern and Central Europe* Helsinki, 1989.

Porteous, A. *Forest Folklore* London, 1928.

Reed, A.W. *Treasury of Maori Folklore* Wellington, 1963.

Rhys, J. *Celtic Folklore* Oxford, 1901.

St Clair, S. *Mysterious Ireland* London, 1994.

Scot, R. *The Discoverie of Witchcraft* London, 1584.

Shuker, K.P.N. *The Unexplained* n.p., 1996.

South, M. I. *Mythical and Fabulous Creatures* New York, 1987.

Spence, L, *British Fairy Origins* London, 1946.

Spence, L, *The Fairy Tradition in Britain* London, 1948.

Spence, L, *The Minor Traditions of British Mythology* London, 1948

Stott, L. *Enchantment of the Trossachs* Milton-of-Aberfoyle, 1992.

Tongue, R.L. *Somerset Folklore* London, 1965.

Trigg, K.B. *Gypsy Demons and Divinities* London, 1975.

Waters, D. *Chinese Mythology* London, 1992.

Wentz, W.Y.E. *The Fairy Faith in Celtic Countries* Gerrards Cross, 1977.

White, C. *History of Irish Fairies* Dublin, 1976.

Westwood., J. *Albion* London 1987

# Index

Adaro, 10
Aegipan, 121
Aengus, 143
Afanc, 10
Agogwe, 10-11
Agriu, 64
Aguane, 11, 139
Ahriman, 39
Ahès, 111
Áine, 11
Alberich, 11
Alcina, 11
Alcyoneus, 64
Algon, 12
Alux, 12
Amazona, 12
Amerant, 64
Ana, 12, 21
Ancho, 12
Andrianoro, 13
Andvari, 13
Angrboda, 64
Annwn, 13, 15, 76
Anuanima, 13
Aoibheall, 13, 32
Apc'Lnic, 14
Apple of Samarkand, 121
Apsaras, 14
Apsari, 14
Apuku, 14
Arak, 14
Araucanian Indians, 133
Ariel, 14

Arthur, 4, 10, 13, 15, 33, 64, 111, 119, 149, 164
Ascapart, 64
Askafroa, 15
Asrai, 15
Atlas, 64
Atua, 15
Auilix, 12
Avalon, 4, 13, 15, 107
Awd Goggie, 15
Ayana, 15

Baba Yaga, 16-17
Bagan, 17
Balan, 64-65
Balor, 64, 143
Balor, 64, 143
Bannik, 17
Banshee, 17
Barabao, 17
Barguest, 18
Battle of Culloden, 145
Bean-nidhe, 18
Befana, 18
Bell, 64, 100, 108
Bendigeidfran, 64
Bendith Y Mamau, 18
Beowulf, 73, 157
Berchte, 18, 50, 79, 95
Berchte, 18, 50, 79, 95
Bergion, 64
Big Grey Man, 19
Bilberry Man, 19
Bindica, 19

Bird Simer, 19
Bjergfolk, 153
Black Annis, 19-20
Bloody-bones, 21
Blue Burches, 21
Blue Maidens, 21
Blue Men of the Minch, 21
Blunderbore, 64
Bocan, 21
Bockmann, 21
Bockschitt, 21
Bodb, 143
Bogey, 22
Boggart, 22, 124
Bogle, 22, 27
Boinn, 143
Bolster, 64
Boruta, 22
Brian Boru, 13
Brollachan, 22
Brounger, 23
Brown, Jane, 23
Brownie, 23, 75, 80-82
Bryn-yr—ellylon, 24
Bucca, 24, 95
Bucky, 24
Bug, 24
Bugaboo, 24
Bujangga, 25
Bull-beggar, 25
Bwbach, 25, 131

Cacce-halde, 26
Cailleach Beara, 26
Cailleach Bheur, 26
Callicantzaros, 27-28
Carabosse, 27
Catez, 27
Cayfor, 27

Centaur, 29-30
Changeling, 29, 31, 156
Charlemagne, 164
Children of Lir, 146
Ching, 31
Chiron, 29
Chu Pa-chiai, 27
Church Grim, 31
Cin, 31
Circe, 151
Ciuthach, 32
Clint's Crags, 32
Cliona, 32
Cluricaune, 32
Coblynau, 32
Cochion, 32
Colbrand, 64
Cormoran, 64
Corn-buck, 33
Corrigan, 33-34, 42, 96
Corwrion, 33
Cottingley fairies, 33
Coulin, 64
Craig-y-ddinas, 35
Crindbel, 143
Crymlyn Lake, 35
Cwm Llwchi Llyn, 35
Cwmsilini Llyn, 35
Cyclops, 35-37
Cyhiraeth, 37
Cynwch, Llyn, 37

Dagda, 143
Dahari, 38
Dahut, 111
Dakini, 38
Dana, 142-143
Danamo, 38
Dark Man, 38

Daughters of the Sun, 38
Davy Jones, 39
Demogorgon, 39
Derrick, 39
Deva, 39, 124
Diana, 151, 172
Diancecht, 143
Dirne-weibel, 39
Dis, 119
Dobie, 40
Dogir, 40
Domovoy, 40
Dondasch, 64
Drac, 40
Druids, 41, 112
Duende, 41
Dullahan, 41
Dunter, 41, 130
Dunvegan Castle, 52
Dwarf, 10-11, 13, 31, 41-42, 44,
    98, 119, 134, 141, 156, 171
Dziwitza, 42
Dôn, 21
DÖppelganger, 40
Eachrais Urlair, 43
Eager, 43
Early, Biddy, 43

Earthman, 43
Edenhall Luck, 43
El Coco, 33
Elemental, 14, 44, 146
Elf, 41, 44-45, 49, 105, 123,
    130, 143, 156, 162
Elf-shot, 46, 125
Elidor, 46
Elima, 46
Ellyllon, 46
Eloko, 47

Eochaidh Ollathair, 143

Eqqo, 47
Exotica, 47
Fachan, 49
Fadet, 49
Fairy Baptism, 51
Fairy, 4-6, 11-15, 18, 25, 27,
    29, 32, 37-40, 43-44, 48-55,
    57, 59, 63, 67, 69, 76-77, 79,
    81-86, 88, 90-91, 95, 97-99,
    104-105, 107, 111-113, 118-
    121, 123-124, 127, 129-132,
    135, 137, 139, 141, 147-148,
    151-153, 157-159, 162-163,
    171-174
Fairy Boy Of Leith, 51
Fairy Chimneys, 51
Fairy Cows, 51
Fairy Cross Plain, 52
Fairy Dog, 52
Fairy Flag, 52
Fairy Food, 53, 86, 151
Fairy Godmother, 53, 172
Fairy Heron, 53
Fairy Hound, 54
Fairy Islands, 54
Fairy Market, 54
Fairy Marriages, 54, 153
Fairy Parlour, 54
Fairy Ring, 55
Fairy Saddle, 55
Fairy Trees, 55
Fankenmannikin, 55
Farfadet, 49
Father Christmas, 55, 82
Faula, 56
Faun, 56
Fauna, 56

Faunus, 56, 144
Fear Dearg, 56
Fenodyree, 56-57, 67
Feriers, 57
Ferishers, 57
Ferracute, 64
Findhorn, 56-57
Finn, 64
Finvarra, 57, 132
Finz-weibel, 57
Fion, 58-59
Flibbertigibbet, 59
Folletto, 59
Fuath, 22, 59, 160
Fudditu, 60
Fujettu, 60

Ga'n, 61
Gahe, 61
Galley-beggar, 61
Galligantus, 64
Gallitrap, 61
Gargantua, 63-64
Geirrod, 64
Gello, 61
Genie, 61, 87
Gervase of Tilbury, 40, 71, 129
Ghille Dubh, 63
Gialout, 63
Giane, 63
Giant of St Michael's Mount, 64
Giant, 19, 31, 37, 55, 59, 62-65, 75, 93, 119, 124, 140, 143, 146, 162
Gitulius, 65
Glaistig, 67
Glashtyn, 67
Gloriana, 67

Gnome, 57, 66-67
Goatman, 21, 67
Goblin, 21, 24, 27, 67, 69, 75, 127, 134, 151, 171
Goemagot, 63-64
Goibniu, 143
Goldemar, 69, 160
Gorgon, 69-70
Gorska, 69
Gossamer, 71
Grac'Hed Coz, 71
Grant, 71
Green Children, 71
Green Ladies, 71
Green Man, 72-73
Gremlin, 73
Grendel, 73
Grey Man, 19, 73
Gruagach, 73, 75
Gryla, 74-75
Gubich, 75
Gugwes, 75
Gunna, 75
Guy of Warwick, 51, 64
Gwrach Y Rhibyn, 76
Gwragged Annwn, 76
Gwyllion, 76
Gwyn Ap Nudd, 4, 53, 76
Gyre-carlin, 76

Harlequin, 77, 164, 173
Hedley Kow, 78-79
Heimchen, 79
Heizemänn, 79
Herla, 79-80, 150
Herne The Hunter, 80
Heurodys, 120
Hibla-bashi, 80
Hippocentaur, 29

Hob, 80-81, 99
Hobbit, 80
Hobgoblin, 80-81, 173
Hobthrust, 80-81
Holda, 18, 50, 81-82
Holiburn, 64
Homesprite, 12, 14, 22, 31, 40-
    41, 65, 67, 69, 79, 82, 90, 95,
    103, 117, 131, 152, 157, 159
Hooper, 82
Hop O' My Thumb, 82
Horse And Hattock, 82
Hotei, 82
Hrothgar, 73
Hrungir, 64
Hsien, 82
Hugon, 83
Huldre-folk, 82
Humpty Dumpty, 83
Huon Of Bordeaux, 83
Huron Indians, 146
Hyena Man, 83
Hylde-moer, 55
Hylde-vinde, 55
Hymir, 64
Härdmandle, 77

HÖgfolk, 81
Ichthyocentaur, 29
Idris, 64
Iele, 84
Ihk'al, 84, 163
Ileana, 84
Incubus, 84
Iron, 6, 10, 29, 76, 85, 123

Jack-in-the-green, 86
Jack O' Legs, 65
Jalpari, 86

Jarnsaxa, 65
JashtesmÉ, 86
Jeffries, Anne, 86
Jenny Greenteeth, 86
Jersey Devil, 87
Jinn, 38, 51, 61, 87, 89
Joint-eater, 87-88
Jola Sveinar, 88
Jones, Edward, 88
Judy, 88
Julbuk, 88
Julenisse, 88
Jultomte, 88

Kachina, 89
Kaf, 89
Kahui-a-tipua, 89
Kakamora, 89
Kakangora, 89
Kalkadoon, 89
Kappa, 89
Katzenveit, 90
Kaukas, 90
Keely, John, 90
Kelpie, 67, 90
Kensington Gardens, 90, 124
Keshalyi, 91
King Avallo, 15
Kirata, 91
Kirk, Robert, 91, 173
Kirk Andreas, 93
Kirk, 3, 40, 50, 53, 87, 91, 93,
    118, 142, 173
Kirnis, 93
Kisimbi, 93
Klaubauf, 93
Klaubauterman, 93
Klwakwe, 93
Knecht Ruprecht, 92-93, 95

Knocker, 94-95
Kobold, 65, 95
Kodin-haltia, 95
Kopuwai, 95
Korrigan, 96
Kratti, 96
Kris Kringle, 56
Krsaspa, 96
Kucda-qa, 96
Kunal-trow, 96
Kâf, 124

La Dormette, 139
La Plata Dwarfs, 98
Lamia, 97
Lamia Of The Sea, 97
Laminak, 97
Lancelot, 4
Lane, Lough, 97
Latona, 151
Laurin, 98
Lauru, 98
Lazy Lawrence, 98
LeannÁn SÍ, 99
Leprechaun, 32, 99
Leshy, 99
Lile Hob, 99
Lipsipsip, 99
Lisunka, 99
Little Men In Cars, 100
Little Red Men, 100
Little Spirits, 100
Loireag, 100
Loki, 13, 44, 64
Lolok, 100
Londonderry Air, 100
Lorelei, 100-101
Lugh, 64, 143
Luot-chozjik, 101

Lurline, 101
Luter, 65
Lutin, 101

Mab, 103, 118-119, 132
Maelor, 65
Maero, 89, 95, 103, 123, 147
Maimune, 104
Majahaldjas, 103
Malekin, 103
Mamucca, 104
Man in the Moon, 104
Man Of Hunger, 104
Mannegishi, 105
Manannan, 143
Mara, 105
Margot, 105
Massariol, 105
May Day, 35, 105
Maya, 12
Mazikin, 105
Melalo, 105
Melusine, 107
Menehune, 107
Mermaid, 15, 69, 106-109, 115,
    144
Merman, 10, 109
Metshänhaltia, 109
Metsik, 109
Meylandt, 109
Midsummer Night's Dream,
    29, 119, 130, 135, 151
Midwife to the Fairies, 111
Moel Fama, 111
Monaciello, 111
Morgan, 12, 15, 50, 110-112,
    115, 148

Morgan Le Fay, 12, 15, 50, 110-111, 148
Morgante, 65
Morozko, 112
Morrigan, 143
Mother of Trees, 112
Mourie, 112
Muma Padura, 112
Mumpoker, 112
Muryan, 112
Musgrave Family, 43
Myddfai, Physicians of, 113
Mära-halddo, 105
Naga, 114
Naranarayana, 14
Narbrooi, 114
Nat, 114
Negroes of the Water, 114
Nereid, 47, 115, 118, 132-133
Nevyn, 115
Niamh, 150
Nickur, 115
Niddy Noddy, 55
Nimble Men, 117
Ninnir, 115
Nis, 117
Nix, 77, 116-117
Niägruisar, 115
Njuzu, 117
Nodens, 76
Nootka Indians, 130
Nork, 117
Nuada, 143
Nuckelavee, 117
Nurses To Fairies, 118
Nymph, 14, 37, 88, 93, 100-101, 115, 118, 147, 156

O'Shea, Michael, 120

Oberon, 11, 67, 83, 91, 118-119, 137, 151
Og, 63
Ogma, 143
Ogo Hole, 119
Ogre, 73, 75, 83, 95, 119-120
Olyroun, 120
Omang, 120
Onocentaur, 29
Orang Bunyi, 120
Orcullo, 120
Orcus, 119
Orfeo, 120, 129
Orianda, 120
Oriande, 120
Ox-foot Stone, 51

Pamarindo, 121
Pan, 27, 59, 90, 121-122, 124, 140, 144, 157
Papa, 121
Parana Dwarfs, 121
Pari-banou, 121
Patupaiarehe, 123
Pavaro, 123
Pech, 123, 125
Peg Fowler, 123
Peg O'Nell, 123
Peggy Wi' T'Lanthorn, 123-124
Peri, 51, 124, 141
Peter Pan, 59, 90, 124
Phi, 124
Picktree-brag, 125
Picts, 123
Pig Fairy, 127
Pigwiggin, 118
Pilwiz, 21, 125
Pisaca, 127, 134
Pixy, 39, 126-127, 173

Planetaroi, 27
Pluto, 119, 127, 129-130
Pluto, 119, 127, 129-130
Polednice, 129
Polevlk, 129
Polong, 129
Pooka, 128-129
Portune, 129
Powrie, 130
Prometheus, 130
Proserpine, 118, 129-130, 132
Prospero, 14
Puck-hairy, 130
Puck, 118, 130, 173
Pukmis, 130
Pwca, 25, 131

Qatu, 132
Quaternica, 132
Queen of the Fairies
   (Connacht), 132

Queen of the Fairies, 12, 32,
   103, 105, 132, 147, 149, 152
Queen of the Mountains, 132
Queen of the Shore, 97, 133
Quetronamun, 133

Rahm, Peter, 134
Raiko, 145
Raksa, 134, 171
Ranzau, Countess Von, 134
Rapunzel, 135
Rarohenga, 135
Red-haired Man, 135
Redcap, 135
Rhosddu, Llyn, 135
Rience, 65
Robin Hood, 65, 137

Robin Roundcap, 137
Roland, 64, 164
Romany Lore, 105, 132
Romany, 91, 105, 132
Rubenzal, 137
Rumpelstiltskin, 137, 152
Rusalka, 6, 138

Salbanello, 139
Salgfraulein, 139
Salvanello, 139
Salvano, 139
Samanach, 139
Samodiva, 139
Sandman, 139
Santa Claus, 55-56
Saucy Jack, 55
Scazzamurieddu, 140
Scrattel, 140
Sea-trow, 140
Seal-folk, 140
Seehirt, 140
Seelie Court, 141
Shambhala, 7, 9
Shasta, Mount, 141
Shean, 141
Sheba, Queen of, 141
Shellycoat, 142
Shinseen, 142
Shock, 142, 151
Shoney, 142
Sibille, 142
Sidh, 142-143, 153
Sigmund Freud, 59
Sigvard Fostre, 143
Silen, 143
Silvan, 144
Silvanus, 144
Siren, 143-144

Skogsra, 144
Skree, 145
Sky Spirits, 145
Sorcha, 145
Spider-woman, 145
Spriggan, 145
St Nicholas, 55
Star Spirits, 145
Strentu, 146
Sun Hou-tzu, 127
Surt, 65
Swan Maidens, 146
Sylph, 14, 146
Sylvester, 146

Tahmuras, 124
Talon-haltija, 147
Tam Lin, 147-148
Tamara, 147
Tarbat, 162
Tarogolo, 148
Tarw, Llyn, 148
Taterman, 148
Tawa-o-hoi, 147
Teind, 148-149
Terdelaschoye, 148
Thiazi, 65
Thomas The Rhymer, 53, 148-
    150
Thrummy-cap, 150
Thrym, 65
Thunderbore, 65
Tiddy-mun, 150, 171
Titania, 119, 132, 151
Tokoloshe, 151
Tom-na-hurich Hill, 151
Tom Thumb, 53, 118, 151
Tom-tit-tot, 137, 152
Tomalin, 151

Tomte, 152
Tooth Fairy, 152
Trasgu, 152
Trebegean, 65
Triunnis Nagelwch, 152
Troll, 134, 152-153, 159
Trow, 96, 140, 153-154
Tuatha Dé Danaan, 11, 142-
    143, 153
Turehu, 135, 153
Tweedie, 153, 155
Tylwyth Teg, 50, 155

Ucakijana, 156
Uiirksak, 156
Ulk, 156
Undine, 156
Unseelie Court, 156
Urchin, 157
Urgan, 157
Urganda, 157
Urisk, 23, 32, 157
Ursitory, 157

Vanadevata, 158
Vazila, 158
Ved, 158
Vedenhaltia, 158
Vesna, 158
Vette, 158
Vila, 159
Vitra, 159
Vittore, 159
Vivian, 159
Vodyany, 159
Vollmar, 69, 160
Vollmar, 69, 160
Vough, 160

Wachholder, Frau, 161
Wachilt, 161
Wade, 64-65, 162
Wag at the Wa', 161
Waldgeister, 161
Wanagemeswak, 161
Wang Chih, 162
Watermaids, 161
Wayland, 65, 161-162
Wells, 162
Wendi, 163
Wight, 112, 163
Wild Edric, 163
Wild Hunt, 77, 80, 163
Wild Maidens, 164
Wild Men, 164
Wild Women, 165
Will O' The Wisp, 127, 130,
   165
Williams, Edward, 165
Witches, 81, 165, 174
Wodel, 167
Wodewose, 164, 167
Wokulo, 167
Woman of the Mist, 167
Wood-wife, 57, 169-170
Woodfolk, 167
Woodland Maidens, 167
Wryneck, 170
Wulver, 170
Wut-ia, 170

Xana, 171
Xelua, 65

Yadu, 134
Yaksa, 171
Yaktayvia, 141, 171
Yaktayvia, 141, 171

Yarthkin, 171
Yellow Dwarf, 171
Ymir, 65
Yosei, 171
Yspadadden, 63, 65
Yspadadden Penkawr, 63
Yvonne, 171

Zina, 172
Zip, 172
Zlata Baba, 172
Zmej, 172
Zorphee, 172

# A selection of other Capall Bann titles. Free catalogue available.

## The Fairies in the Irish Tradition  by Molly Gowen

A comprehensive study of the fairy nature and its manifestations in the Irish tradition, illustrated with stories and legends and illuminated with superb artwork. Contents include: Fairy Nature - fallen angels, elementals and ghosts; Fairies in the Landscape; The Banshee; History of the Sidhe; the Fairy Doctor; Tir na nOg; magical animals, the Pooka, the King of Cats and Demon Dogs. Superb illustrations by Lavinia Hamer. ISBN 186163 0859

## Wondrous Land - The Faery Faith of Ireland  by Kay Mullin

Dr Kay Mullin, a clinical psychologist by profession, was introduced to the world of faery by spirit channelled through a medium. That meeting led to extensive research in Ireland, collecting stories both old and new - from people who not only know of faeries, but see them too - in the land so long associated with them. The result is this wonderful book. The text is complemented with lyrical poetry from an Irish seer, and exquisite drawings. The faery faith is real, alive and growing in Ireland. Illustrated by Cormac Figgis. *"....a delight...a living, personal story from the Atlantic edge..." 3rd Stone*  ISBN  186163 010 7       £10.95              Illustrated

## Real Fairies  by David Tame

Encounters with fairies seem to be increasing. This book relates the experiences of many people, some famous (such as BBC presenter Valerie Singleton), some clairvoyant, some everyday, who have seen and met members of the fairy kingdom. It appears that our world and theirs are drawing closer together again and it is possible for more and more people to see what we have been told by some for generations does not exist. ISBN  186163 0719

## The Mythology of the Mermaid and Her Kin  by Marc Potts

Explores the origin of Mermaids and Mermen. Sea deities, especially those depicted as being fish-tailed are explored, as is the mythology of woman's association with water. The folklore of mermaids is related, especially from Britain and Northern Europe, with relevant examples from other parts of the world. Other topics related include: the mermaid's image in bestiaries, the mermaid and the Christian church, carvings and heraldry, recorded sightings and captures, the seal/siren explanation, mermaid hoaxes and the mermaids' image today.The text is illustrated by Marc's superb paintings - for an example see the superb covers of *'The Wildwood King'* and *'The Spirits of the Elements'* series he did for us. ISBN 18663 0395

## Spirits of the Earth  by Jaq D Hawkins

This is the first volume in the Spirits of the Earth series in which Jaq D Hawkins shares an understanding of the basic nature of elemental spirits with her readers. Within each volume, Ms. Hawkins explains to us the nature of the element, types of spirits associated with each element, and correspondences in magical thought as well as rituals and divination methods in natural magic. Included in *Spirits of the Earth* are the types of natural objects, and sometimes man-made objects, which attract Earth Spirit inhabitants as well as methods to see or communicate with these elemental spirits, places of worship or invocation, and the nature of thought form spirits associated with the Earth element. From fanciful fairies to guardian spirits of stone circles, Spirits of the Earth is a 'must have' for anyone who has an interest in elemental spirits. ISBN 186163 002 6              £8.95

# FREE DETAILED CATALOGUE

A detailed illustrated catalogue is available on request, SAE or International Postal Coupon appreciated. Titles are available direct from Capall Bann, post free in the UK (cheque or PO with order) or from good bookshops and specialist outlets. Titles currently available include:

Angels and Goddesses - Celtic Christianity & Paganism by Michael Howard
Arthur - The Legend Unveiled by C Johnson & E Lung
Auguries and Omens - The Magical Lore of Birds by Yvonne Aburrow
Book of the Veil The by Peter Paddon
Caer Sidhe - Celtic Astrology and Astronomy by Michael Bayley
Call of the Horned Piper by Nigel Jackson
Celtic Lore & Druidic Ritual by Rhiannon Ryall
Compleat Vampyre - The Vampyre Shaman: Werewolves & Witchery by Nigel Jackson
Crystal Clear - A Guide to Quartz Crystal by Jennifer Dent
Earth Dance - A Year of Pagan Rituals by Jan Brodie
Earth Harmony - Places of Power, Holiness and Healing by Nigel Pennick
Earth Magic by Margaret McArthur
Enchanted Forest - The Magical Lore of Trees by Yvonne Aburrow
Familiars - Animal Powers of Britain by Anna Franklin
Healing Homes by Jennifer Dent
Herbcraft - Shamanic & Ritual Use of Herbs by Susan Lavender & Anna Franklin
In Search of Herne the Hunter by Eric Fitch
Kecks, Keddles & Kesh by Michael Bayley
Living Tarot by Ann Walker
Magical Incenses and Perfumes by Jan Brodie
Magical Lore of Cats by Marion Davies
Magical Lore of Herbs by Marion Davies
Masks of Misrule - The Horned God & His Cult in Europe by Nigel Jackson
Mysteries of the Runes by Michael Howard
Oracle of Geomancy by Nigel Pennick
Patchwork of Magic by Julia Day
Pathworking - A Practical Book of Guided Meditations by Pete Jennings
Pickingill Papers - The Origins of Gardnerian Wicca by Michael Howard
Psychic Animals by Dennis Bardens
Psychic Self Defence - Real Solutions by Jan Brodie
Runic Astrology by Nigel Pennick
Sacred Animals by Gordon MacLellan
Sacred Grove - The Mysteries of the Forest by Yvonne Aburrow
Sacred Geometry by Nigel Pennick
Sacred Lore of Horses The by Marion Davies
Sacred Ring - Pagan Origins British Folk Festivals & Customs by Michael Howard
Seasonal Magic - Diary of a Village Witch by Paddy Slade
Secret Places of the Goddess by Philip Heselton
Talking to the Earth by Gordon Maclellan
Taming the Wolf - Full Moon Meditations by Steve Hounsome
The Goddess Year by Nigel Pennick & Helen Field
West Country Wicca by Rhiannon Ryall
Witches of Oz The by Matthew & Julia Phillips

Capall Bann is owned and run by people actively involved in many of the areas in which we publish. Our list is expanding rapidly so do contact us for details on the latest releases.

**Capall Bann Publishing, Freshfields, Chieveley, Berks, RG20 8TF**